The Shropshire Union Railway

Stafford to Shrewsbury including the Coalport Branch

by
Bob Yate

THE OAKWOOD PRESS

© Oakwood Press & Bob Yate 2003

British Library Cataloguing in Publication Data
A Record for this book is available from the British Library
ISBN 0 85361 613 2

Typeset by Oakwood Graphics.
Repro by Ford Graphics, Ringwood, Hants.
Printed by Cambrian Printers, Aberystwyth, Ceredigion.

Cast-iron notice board for the Great Western and London & North Western Railways gives warning to trespassers on railway property at Shrewsbury in 1956. *R.M. Casserley*

Front cover: Class '4' Fairburn 2-6-4T No. 42247 on the 5.40 pm Stafford-Wellington passenger train getting under way from its stop at Newport on 29th August, 1964.
Michael Mensing

Rear cover, top: One of the more unusual workings in latter years was a Crewe to Willesden parcels train, which travelled westwards from Crewe, then down through Market Drayton to Wellington, thence along the SUR to Stafford. Frequently it was hauled by a Stanier Pacific, and here is shown 'Princess Coronation' class No. 46248 *City of Leeds*, in rather grubby maroon livery, passing near Haughton in the summer of 1964. *E. Talbot*

Rear cover, bottom: A fine view of BR Standard class '5' 4-6-0 No. 73053 with the 4.04 pm Stafford to Shrewsbury train west of Gnosall on 29th August, 1964. *Michael Mensing*

Published by The Oakwood Press (Usk), P.O. Box 13, Usk, Mon., NP15 1YS.
E-mail: oakwood-press@dial.pipex.com
Website: www.oakwood-press.dial.pipex.com

Contents

Abbreviations

The following abbreviations are used throughout the text:

GJR	Grand Junction Railway
GNR	Great Northern Railway
GWR	Great Western Railway
L&BR	London & Birmingham Railway
LMSR	London, Midland & Scottish Railway
LNWR	London & North Western Railway
OWWR	Oxford, Worcester & Wolverhampton Railway
PSNWR	Potteries, Shrewsbury & North Wales Railway
S&BR	Shrewsbury & Birmingham Railway
S&MR	Shropshire & Montgomeryshire Railway
SUR	Shropshire Union Railway
SUR&CC	Shropshire Union Railways & Canal Company

Note that the correct title for the SUR&CC includes 'railways' in the plural, even if the official company notices did not always manage to spell it thus! (*See pages 15 and 30.*)

Introduction

Several canal companies converted their canals into railways during the early 19th century, and others were purchased by railway companies and subsequently converted. However, the Shropshire Union Railway (SUR), running from Stafford to Shrewsbury, was unusual in that it was one of the few public railways in Britain to have been built as such by an erstwhile canal company. The Monmouthshire Railway & Canal Company was probably the only other to achieve this distinction. Some canal companies did admittedly build small, local goods lines mainly as feeders to their wharves. The Manchester Ship Canal Railway is probably the largest example of this practice, but falls short of being a public railway, as no public passenger service was operated.

Around one-third of the route mileage of the SUR was a joint line, primarily for financial reasons, but also at the behest of Parliament, which was concerned at the proliferation of railway schemes in the area. Its partner, the Shrewsbury & Birmingham Railway (S&BR) never reached its destination of Birmingham, and was inevitably involved in the competitive struggle for railways around Wolverhampton. As the London & North Western Railway (LNWR) not only operated the SUR from its opening, but also oversaw its construction, it was perhaps inevitable that the forceful character of its General Manager, Captain Mark Huish, would be evident in its dealings with the S&BR, and subsequently with its successor, the Great Western Railway (GWR).

These troublesome times eventually gave way to a more relaxed period in the railway's history, when it gave good service to its customers and constantly sought ways to improve its freight and passenger services. The area was rich in mineral resources, as well as manufacturing enterprise, and the railway played its part through both peacetime and wartime in promoting these activities. Its location meant that although it was never a congested traffic route, it was a very useful diversionary route during emergencies.

In the 1960s, passenger and freight traffic was falling both nationally and locally, as the result of several large businesses closing. There was an air of inevitability of closure for the line from Stafford to Wellington. However, electrification work on the West Coast main line once more brought new life to the line, as it again played its valuable role as a diversionary route. But although this just delayed the inevitable, the line closed in very gradual stages, not completely between Stafford and Wellington until 1991. The future for the remaining section, the joint line from Wellington to Shrewsbury, appears assured, even if the intermediate stations have gone.

Little trace remains of the one branch line, to Coalport, but its history is rooted in the industrial revolution, and is told here.

LOCATION MAP

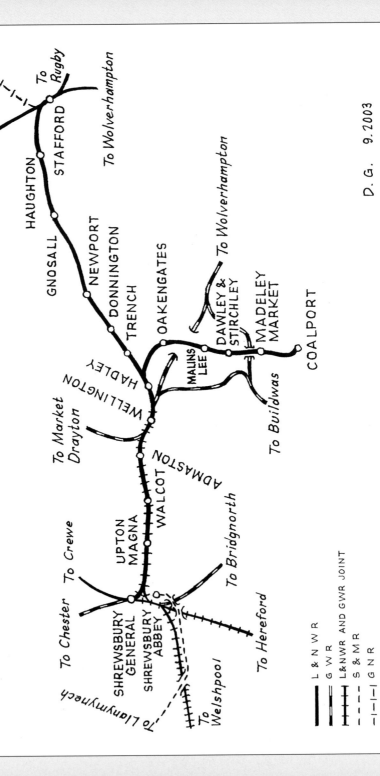

To Crewe
To Uttoxeter
To Rugby
STAFFORD
HAUGHTON
To Wolverhampton
GNOSALL
NEWPORT
DONNINGTON
TRENCH
OAKENGATES
To Wolverhampton
DAWLEY & STIRCHLEY
MALINS LEE
MADELEY MARKET
COALPORT
HADLEY
WELLINGTON
To Buildwas
To Market Drayton
ADMASTON
WALCOT
UPTON MAGNA
To Bridgnorth
To Crewe
To Chester
SHREWSBURY GENERAL
SHREWSBURY ABBEY
To Hereford
To Llanymynech
To Welshpool

L & N W R
G W R
L&NWR AND GWR JOINT
S & M R
G N R

D. G.   9.2003

Chapter One

Shropshire Union - The Origins

The Shropshire Union Railways and Canal Company was formed in 1846 from an amalgamation of four canal companies, to provide a direct route from the industrial West Midlands to the North of England, North Wales, and an export route via the Mersey seaports. In addition, from its inception the company intended to open 155 miles of railways, either by conversion of its own canals or building new lines, having recognised that they could not compete with the speed of the railways. Details of the four companies involved follow.

The Chester Canal. Opened in 1779 from Chester to Nantwich. A branch from Barbridge Junction (four miles north of Nantwich) to Middlewich was started in July 1827, with Thomas Telford as Engineer, and opened on 1st September, 1835.

The Ellesmere Canal. This canal was originally intended to run from Shrewsbury to Chester and on to the Mersey at a place called Netherpool (later renamed Ellesmere Port). Thus, the intention was to link the navigable portions of the Severn, the Dee and the Mersey, and to provide a through route from the Midlands and Mid-Wales to the sea. It initially ignored the Chester Canal, as this had become very run down by the 1790s. There were to be branches to the east to Whitchurch, to the west to Brymbo and Llangollen, and to the south-west to Llanymynech (meeting the Montgomeryshire Canal in 1797). William Jessop was appointed as Engineer, with Thomas Telford as his deputy. However, the scale of problems in building Telford's viaducts at Chirk and Pontcysyllte seriously delayed the section continuing northwards towards Chester, such that it was eventually abandoned. Instead, the Whitchurch branch was continued past Whitchurch to join the Chester Canal at Hurleston Junction, two miles north of Nantwich. Furthermore, the southern section to Shrewsbury was abandoned at a wharf in the middle of fields at Weston Lullingfields. Meanwhile, the northernmost section of this canal, known as 'The Wirral Line', running from Chester to the River Mersey at Netherpool, opened on 1st July, 1795. The remainder of the canal was eventually completed, with the 'main line' to Hurleston Junction opening in 1805, and branches to Llanymynech (1796), Prees (1806), Whitchurch, which had been bypassed by the 'main line' (1808), and Llangollen (1808).

Thereafter, relations between the Ellesmere and Chester canals were so interdependent, that an amalgamation was inevitable. Consequently, on 1st July, 1813, these two canals became the Ellesmere and Chester Canal Company.

In May 1826, the enabling Act was passed for the *Birmingham and Liverpool Junction Canal*. It is noteworthy that the Act for the Liverpool and Manchester Railway was passed in the same Parliamentary session. The Act authorised a canal from Autherley Junction (where it joined the Staffordshire and Worcestershire Canal) to Nantwich, thus completing the through route from the Midlands to the sea. Thomas Telford was appointed as Principal Engineer, with

Telford spent much time and money trying to overcome the geographical difficulties on the Llangollen Canal. One of his major achievements was the iron aqueduct crossing the River Dee at Pontcysyllte, completed in 1805. The iron trough is supported on 19 stone piers, measures over 1,000 ft-long, and at its highest is 127 ft-tall over the valley bottom.   *Author*

The Birmingham & Liverpool Junction Canal crossed Watling Street (now the A5) on an iron aqueduct at Stretton, near Brewood in Staffordshire. Thomas Telford's magnificent edifice still stands, proudly bearing his name and the date 1832. Unfortunately, although the canal (which later became the SUR&CC's 'main line canal') was finished in that year, because of repeated collapses of embankment and cuttings, it was not finally opened throughout until 1835.   *Author*

Alexander Easton as Resident Engineer. At this time, Telford was also working on the London to Holyhead road (1815-1830), the shortening and straightening of James Brindley's original Birmingham Canal Navigation through the Black Country (completed in 1829), and was consulting engineer on the Trent and Mersey Canal. Telford had decided to make the Birmingham and Liverpool Canal as straight and free of locks as possible, using cuttings and embankments (as he had done on the Birmingham Canal). This coincided with the methods used in railway construction, but was designed to make the canal more competitive in the face of the new fangled railways. However, he was beset with constructional problems as his cuttings and embankments were considerably larger than anything tackled before. Despite numerous slippages, the canal was nearly ready for opening in 1832, only to suffer further collapses. Telford's health was now failing, and the canal committee was concerned that the work was not proceeding in the expected manner. Consequently, William Cubitt was appointed as company Engineer, and finally managed to solve the constructional problems, mostly caused by the steepness of the sides of the embankments and cuttings. The canal finally opened on 2nd March, 1835. Meanwhile, Telford had died on 2nd September, 1834 aged 77, and so never saw his canal completed.

An Act of 1827 also authorised a branch from Norbury Junction through Newport, to link with the Shrewsbury Canal at Wappenshall (1½ miles north of Wellington). Construction of this branch of just over 10 miles was initially delayed, but eventually it was opened on 12th January, 1832. A short branch, known as the Humber Arm, was provided on to the Duke of Sutherland's land at Lubstree Wharf near Donnington. Including the link to the Shrewsbury Canal, the final cost of the Birmingham and Liverpool Junction Canal was £800,000, compared to the original authorised capital of £400,000 with a £100,000 reserve.

The fourth component of the SUR&CC was the *Shrewsbury Canal*, which ran from wharves adjacent to the River Severn at Shrewsbury, and served the iron and coal fields of East Shropshire from the west. The enabling Act for this company was passed in 1793, and in August 1793 Josiah Clowes was appointed as Engineer. However, he died in early 1795 and was replaced by Thomas Telford, who at that time was part time Surveyor of Public Works for Shropshire, and also assistant to William Jessop on the Ellesmere Canal (as above). The canal was opened in stages from 1794 until 1797. During this period, the short (one mile) Wombridge Canal was also acquired by the Shrewsbury Canal company. A General Assembly of the company, held at the Raven Hotel, Shrewsbury in October 1826 authorised the branch of the Birmingham and Liverpool Junction Canal from Norbury Junction to be joined to the Shrewsbury Canal, thereby linking it into the remainder of the network.

The sequence of events was as follows:

1st July, 1813 - Ellesmere Canal Company and Chester Canal Company amalgamated to form the Ellesmere and Chester Canal Company.

1st May, 1845 - Ellesmere and Chester Canal Company amalgamated with the Birmingham and Liverpool Junction Canal Company, taking the name of the former company.

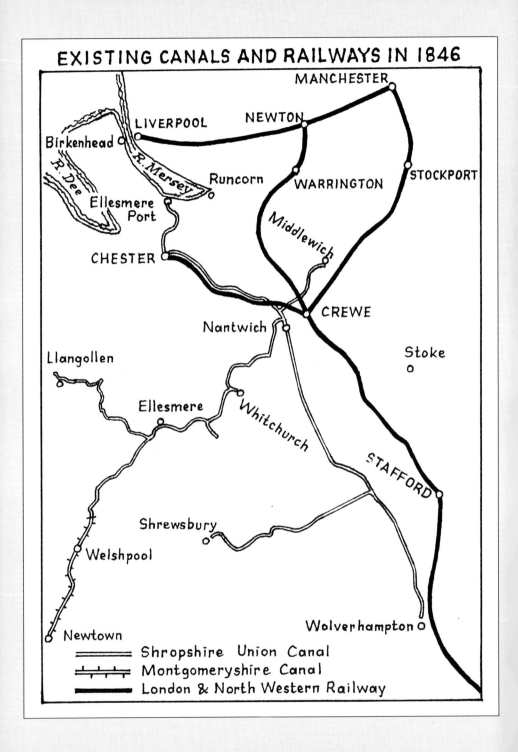

EXISTING CANALS AND RAILWAYS IN 1846

MANCHESTER

LIVERPOOL NEWTON

Birkenhead

R. Dee

R. Mersey

Runcorn WARRINGTON STOCKPORT

Ellesmere Port

Middlewich

CHESTER CREWE

Nantwich Stoke

Llangollen

Ellesmere Whitchurch STAFFORD

Shrewsbury

Welshpool

Newtown Wolverhampton

Shropshire Union Canal
Montgomeryshire Canal
London & North Western Railway

Telford's earlier aqueduct over the River Ceiriog at Chirk was completed in 1801, and represents an earlier design, with the iron trough being carried on a masonry viaduct comprising 10 arches. The later railway viaduct, behind, was constructed some 40 years later for the Shrewsbury & Chester Railway and if anything heightens the drama of the earlier construction. *Author*

3rd August, 1846 - The enlarged Ellesmere and Chester Canal Company changed its name to the Shropshire Union Railways and Canal Company.

3rd August, 1846 - The SUR&CC acquired the Shrewsbury Canal Company, and announced plans to build 155 miles of railways, including conversion of most of its canal routes. The Subscription Share Capital of the SUR&CC was £3.3 million, with a further £1.1 million in reserve, if needed. In order to attract such a vast amount of capital, the SUR&CC displayed its best credentials, appointing the Earl of Powis as Chairman from amongst its distinguished Directors, which included Lord Stafford. A complete list of the Directors is given in *Appendix One*.

However, as can be seen from the above events, the enlarged Ellesmere and Chester Canal Company had already anticipated its role in future railways. Plans were deposited at Shropshire and Staffordshire County Courts on 29th November, 1845 (the latter 'at forty-five minutes after eight o'clock in the afternoon') for the following routes:

Shrewsbury to Stafford using the bed of the Newport Branch Canal between Preston Boats (near Shrewsbury) and Norbury Junction.

Calveley (near Chester) to Oxley (near Wolverhampton) using the canal bed of the Ellesmere & Chester almost entirely.

Newtown to Chester using the canal beds of the Ellesmere & Chester's Llanymynech branch and the Montgomeryshire Canal to Newtown (even though the eastern arm of this canal was not acquired by the SUR&CC until 1847).

The next day, 30th November, 1845, plans were deposited for the SUR line from Stafford to Shrewsbury, with the route via Wellington largely as built. However, in the plans the line divided into two single lines just north of Abbey Foregate. One line turned southwards for one furlong, on the approximate alignment of the later 'Abbey Curve' but passing through the site of today's Shrewsbury Town football ground to reach the terminus near the English Bridge. The other line curved northwards for just over a furlong to reach the SUR&CC canal basin, on the site of what was later to become the Howard Street goods depot. This plan was changed after agreement with the Shrewsbury & Chester Railway, and the Shrewsbury & Hereford Railway, to provide the joint station that was eventually built. The SUR running line was correspondingly altered to pass to the north of Abbey Foregate, but the line to the SUR&CC canal basin was not built until 1858, and then on a different alignment.

The plans also included branches from Gnosall to the Grand Junction Railway at Norton Bridge (six miles north of Stafford), and from there to a junction with the North Staffordshire Railway at Stone (although this was conditional on the North Staffordshire Railway not building the line itself from Stone to Norton Bridge). These parts of the scheme were quietly allowed to be forgotten, but the latter was eventually built by the North Staffordshire Railway in 1852. The engineers for this plan were Robert Stephenson and William Baker. It will be noted that the above dates were not simply coincidental, as the route was authorised by Act of Parliament (Acts 9 & 10, Vict. Chapter 323) on the same day as incorporation of the SUR&CC, on 3rd August, 1846.

Looking south at Norbury Junction, with the SUR&CC 'main line' to Wolverhampton straight ahead. The Newport branch turned off to the right (behind the tree in the photo), but is now blocked after some 200 yards. An important junction and maintenance depot on the canal, many of the original buildings are still in use, albeit in connection with the leisure cruising business today.   *Author*

Chapter Two

Alternative Schemes

This story really began in the 'Railway Mania' of the 1840s during which time the railway system of Great Britain grew at a terrific pace. In most cases, railways were of entirely new construction, but the SUR&CC was not the only company to consider conversion of canals into railways. Eventually, around 2,000 miles of canals were thus converted throughout the country. Railways also absorbed canals so as to provide feeders to their systems and also to control competition from the canal owners. Locally, for example, the North Staffordshire Railway absorbed the Trent & Mersey Navigation in 1846. In the same year, the Birmingham Canals Navigation was leased by the London & Birmingham Railway (and its successor, the LNWR).

Therefore, before proceeding with our story, mention must be made of other routes that had been proposed at earlier dates to link Shrewsbury to Stafford and Wolverhampton. As will be seen, some of these proposals came to nothing, whilst others had a bearing on the final construction, or formed part of these lines.

During the 1830s, Ireland was seen as a growth market for English goods, with the reciprocal trade in agricultural produce as a natural result. New routes were being considered for this traffic, and one small harbour at Porth Dynlleyn (on the north-western side of the Lleyn peninsula, near Nefyn) was favoured. An independent London proposal was made in 1835 via Worcester and Shrewsbury, but nothing more was heard. A year later, Charles Vignoles surveyed a similar route, plus two more this time both leaving the Grand Junction Railway (GJR) at Wolverhampton and travelling via Ironbridge to Shrewsbury, where they diverged. One went via Ellesmere, then along the Dee and Treweryn valleys passing Llangollen, Bala, Trawsfynydd and Porthmadog. The other was routed through Welshpool then along the upper Severn Valley via Newtown, Machynlleth and Dolgellau to Porthmadog. However, the following year, in 1837, Brunel considered a broad gauge route to Porth Dynlleyn, and Vignoles surveyed further routes on his behalf. One went from Wolverhampton via Newport and Market Drayton rejoining his earlier route at Tetch Hill, just outside Ellesmere. All of this effort was eventually frustrated when the Admiralty announced that the development of Porth Dynlleyn was impractical.

An engineer's report and plans were deposited on 1st March, 1839 by Joseph Locke on behalf of the GJR for a railway from the GJR at Bushbury (Wolverhampton) to Shrewsbury. Nothing more was heard of this scheme.

Three interesting plans were deposited on 30th November, 1844. The first two were by Joseph Locke on behalf of the GJR, for a line from Stafford to Shrewsbury. However, Locke's route from Stafford seems to have suffered some change during his survey, as he wrote on 11th March, 1844: 'I send tonight to Huish (Mark Huish, General Manager of the GJR) my report of the Stafford line *as it is*. But I have not got the section on the Shrewsbury side of Penkridge or Stafford . . .' Later he writes, 'I have already stated that the line from

Shrewsbury will unite on the north side of Stafford station'. One of these lines was routed via Wellington, and the other via Oakengates and The Hem (near Shifnal), thence along the Severn Valley. Both of these routes were thrown out of Parliament as a result of lobbying by the London & Birmingham Railway (L&BR). The other route was by the independent Shrewsbury and Wolverhampton, Dudley and Birmingham Railway (shortened on 1st January, 1846 to the Shrewsbury and Birmingham Railway). This plan was backed by the L&BR, so was engineered by Sir George Rennie and Captain W.S. Moorsom, and included extensions to Newtown and Chester. Once again, intense lobbying (this time by the GJR) resulted in this plan being thrown out by Parliament.

On 29th November, 1844 the Shrewsbury, Wolverhampton & South Staffordshire Railway deposited plans prepared by Joseph Locke for a line from Shrewsbury, via Wellington and Oakengates to Wolverhampton. This line proposed joining the GJR (by whom it was supported) at Wolverhampton via a branch on a proposed South Staffordshire Railway, and also included an alternative route via Shifnal, and a branch to Coalbrookdale. Again, lobbying by the L&BR saw this plan fail.

The Shrewsbury to Wolverhampton route was again surveyed, this time with Robert Stephenson and William Baker as engineers. Robert Stephenson had of course to survey the route by horseback, and provided an interim report of his progress from Shrewsbury to the Shrewsbury & Birmingham Railway Directors at Oakengates on 16th August, 1845. He finally completed his survey in September, 1845 and the plan was deposited on 30th November, 1845 for a railway from Shrewsbury to Birmingham, with branches to the GJR at Wolverhampton and to Dudley. This plan was the basis for the line eventually built, although the branch to Dudley was forgotten. The enabling Act received Royal Assent on 3rd August, 1846, which was of course the date of the incorporation of the SUR&CC. For our story, the section from Shrewsbury to Wellington built jointly with the SUR&CC is all that concerns us here.

One further proposal of note is that of yet another concern, the Staffordshire & Shropshire Junction Railway, whose line from the GJR at Stafford to Shrewsbury was detailed in its plan also deposited on 30th November, 1844. Although this was ostensibly an independent concern, and the engineers appointed were J.U. Rastrick and E.J. Maude, it was another GJR scheme and also failed in Parliament.

From these events, it will be seen that there was considerable animosity between the L&BR and the GJR, which mainly stemmed from the support given by the GJR to the broad gauge of the GWR. The GJR was at that time not considered to be in direct competition, and so they were allies. However, the L&BR was in direct competition with the GWR on the Birmingham to London route, amongst others. But matters quickly changed when the GWR started to question the exclusive right of the GJR to Shrewsbury and Merseyside. So much so, that the GJR and L&BR merged along with the Manchester & Birmingham Railway on 16th July, 1846 to form the London & North Western Railway.

Because of the many schemes put forward at this time regarding proposed Midlands railways, the Dalhousie Committee was appointed by the Houses of

Parliament to examine all the schemes and to pronounce on the most viable and desirable schemes. After due consideration, this reported to the Railway Department of the Board of Trade that the S&BR scheme from Shrewsbury to Wolverhampton was preferred because it was independent and the backers were local persons of substantial means.

The efforts of the S&BR to win its original line through to Birmingham have not been described here, as they do not form part of our story. However, the costs involved in fighting its case on both the Shrewsbury to Wolverhampton, and Wolverhampton to Birmingham sections are believed to have amounted to £190,000. So when the time came to start detailed surveying and planning the building of the line from Shrewsbury, the S&BR found that its original funds were somewhat depleted. It found a willing ally in the SUR, so that they could build the line from Wellington to Shrewsbury jointly. As a result, the Bills authorising this line for both the SUR&CC and the S&BR were duly amended in the Committee Room of the House of Commons, and this 10½ mile section of line was officially built under the auspices of the grandly titled 'Shrewsbury and Birmingham and Shropshire Union Railways and Canal Company'.

At this time and for several decades afterwards, additional schemes were put forward for lines which crossed or duplicated the area occupied by the SUR. For the convenience of readers, these are annotated in *Appendix Three*, rather than interrupt the understanding of events as they unfold in our history.

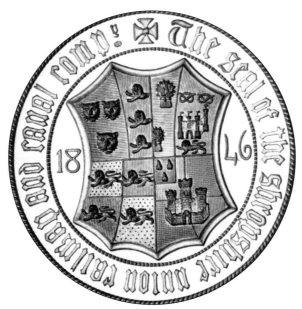

Company seal of Shropshire Union Railways and Canal Company. Note the seal shows the Shropshire Union Railway (singular). *National Railway Museum*

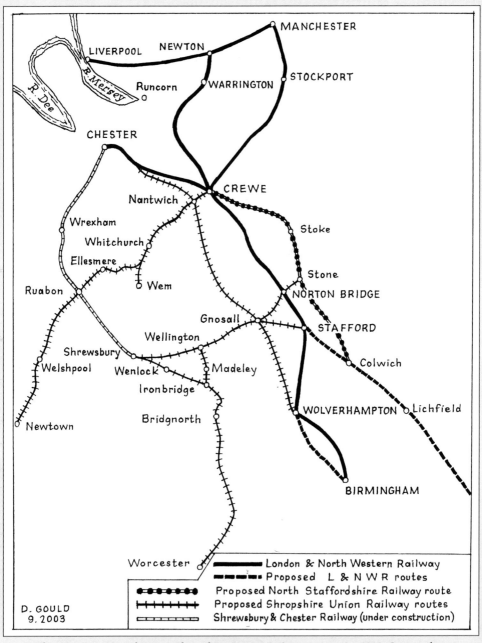

The LNWR and authorised Shropshire Union Railway routes in 1846. Some other authorised routes are shown for completeness.

Chapter Three

Construction

In addition to the surveying of the Stafford-Shrewsbury line during 1845, a survey was also made into the SUR intended 'main line' from Chester to Wolverhampton. This survey was performed by W.A. Provis and W. Cubitt, working under the supervision of the Chief Engineer, Robert Stephenson. It is unlikely that after his initial survey Stephenson spent much time on this project, as his services were then very much in demand all over this country, as well as managing the family locomotive building concern at their Forth Street workshops in Newcastle-upon-Tyne. Provis was the SUR Company Engineer at this time, and so responsibility for the conversion of the canal into railway was clear. Cubitt had been the Principal Engineer from 1832 until the completion of the Birmingham and Liverpool Junction Canal, and so had intimate knowledge of the route and its geological problems.

The survey found that the route of 45 miles and 7 chains from Calveley (just outside Chester, and adjacent to the GJR Crewe-Chester line) to Wolverhampton could be built using the existing canal bed apart from a total of four miles, where entirely new construction would be needed. Running powers would be required over the GJR line from Calveley into Chester. The approach to Wolverhampton was via Oxley, to give a high level station in the town. This showed the influence of Robert Stephenson, who persistently advocated that major stations should be placed at a high level, so that incoming trains would be assisted by the gradient in braking, and departing trains assisted by the gradient in accelerating. The total cost was estimated at £730,000. The plans were put before a Select Committee in 1845 and endorsed by the SUR&CC General Manager, Robert S. Skey, who claimed that 2,000 tons of heavy iron castings could be sent north each week by this route. His evidence claimed that the line should be extended northwards to Birkenhead to preclude transhipment. However, no such plans had been developed by the company at that time. He also opined that the GJR route from Birmingham northwards was 'better calculated' for passenger traffic than the SUR route. This was certainly true, as the only towns passed by the SUR route were Newport (actually at that time still really only a large village) and Market Drayton, and so were unlikely to generate a great deal of passenger traffic. Both of these towns were highly in favour of the proposed route. This is more than can be said for the GJR, which saw this proposed route, and the others proposed by the SUR&CC, as serious rivals. A glance at the map of railways and canals in the region in 1846 will show the reason for the concern expressed by the GJR, which was still a relatively young company and looking to expand in all directions.

Furthermore, the local canal owners, such as the Trent and Mersey and the Staffordshire and Worcestershire, saw this move as an additional threat when one of their own deserted to the opposition!

Nonetheless, as mentioned earlier, the enabling Act was passed on 3rd August, 1846 which also authorised the other proposed SUR lines, for the

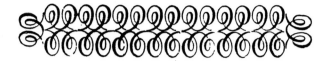

AN

A C T

FOR

Making a Railway from Shrewsbury to Stafford, with a Branch to Stone, and for other Purposes.

[ROYAL ASSENT, AUGUST 3RD, 1846.]

WHEREAS an Act was passed in the seventh and eighth years of the reign of His late Majesty King George the Fourth, intituled "An Act to amend and enlarge the Powers and Provisions of the Acts relating to the Ellesmere and Chester Canal Navigation," whereby certain persons, being proprietors of the Ellesmere and Chester Canals, under certain Acts of Parliament, therein recited and repealed, were reunited into a Company and made a body politic and corporate by the name of "The United Company of Proprietors of the Ellesmere and Chester Canal:"   *Preamble. 7 & 8 Geo. IV.*

And whereas another Act was passed in the eleventh year of the reign of His said late Majesty, intituled "An Act to enable the United Company of Proprietors of the Ellesmere and Chester Canal to make a Reservoir and to establish Vessels for the conveyance of Goods from the Ellesmere Port across the river Mersey, and also to amend and enlarge the powers of the Act relating to the said Canal:"   *11 Geo. IV.*

And whereas another Act was passed in the first year of the reign of Her present Majesty, intituled "An Act to amend and enlarge the Powers of the several Acts relating to the Ellesmere and Chester Canal:"   *1 Vict.*

[57]   B   And

The opening page of the Shropshire Union Railway Act of 3rd August, 1846.

Staffordshire Records Office

engineers had also been Messrs Stephenson, Provis and Cubitt. The Act also established the SUR&CC as a legal entity, and enabled absorption of the Shrewsbury Canal. Meanwhile, the GJR had amalgamated with the Manchester & Birmingham Railway, and the London & Birmingham Railway as from 16th July, 1846 to become the London & North Western Railway. Even before its legal formation, its future Directors had been watching events unfold on the fledgling SUR, and opened talks with that body as soon as it became apparent that they could no longer prevent this rival concern from becoming reality.

The Directors of the SUR&CC decreed that the Stafford to Shrewsbury line was to be built quickly, because 'while it is much required by the district, its construction will not involve any loss of revenue from the canals'.

At the same time the Shrewsbury & Birmingham Railway, partner in the Shrewsbury to Wellington section, had received its authorising Act on the same day as the SUR&CC. Acting in concert, the two railway partners pressed ahead with plans for the construction of the joint railway. To regulate the business affairs of the joint line, a means of management of the construction of the line, as well as operational matters, was embodied in Sections 32 and 33 of the S&BR Act of 3rd August, 1846 which required the formation of a 'Shrewsbury and Wellington Joint Line Committee'. This was duly established, comprising three Directors from each of the two companies, as follows:

For the SUR:	For the S&BR:
The Earl of Powis	Mr Ormesby Gore, MP
Henry Newberry	Hon. R.H. Clive, MP
John Meeson Parsons	Mr Anstice

The first meeting of the Joint Committee was held at the Swan Inn, Wolverhampton on 17th November, 1846 and was also attended by Robert Stephenson, who said that his final plans 'would be ready in a few days'. At this meeting, Robert Stephenson was appointed as Principal Engineer, and William Baker as Chief Engineer for the joint line. Their costs of engineering the line were confirmed as being £450 per mile, exclusive of travelling expenses and the fees of architects and solicitors.

Later, at a meeting of this committee on 22nd February, 1847 a resolution was passed to form a further joint committee, this time dealing with the building and subsequent operation of Shrewsbury General station and the approach lines. This 'Shrewsbury Joint Station Joint Committee' comprised representatives from the SUR, S&BR, Shrewsbury & Chester Railway, and the Shrewsbury & Hereford Railway. Its first meeting was held on 16th April, 1847. In time, with subsequent acquisitions of these constituent companies, the committee comprised only representatives from the LNWR and GWR (after Grouping, the LMSR and GWR).

On 16th April, 1847 a contract was let to the firm of Hammond and Murray for the construction of the joint line from Shrewsbury to Wellington. Thomas Brassey obtained the contract for the Severn Bridge at Shrewsbury station.

For the SUR, George Lee was appointed as Chief Engineer, with a Mr Donaldson as Resident Engineer for the Stafford to Newport section. Subsequently, contracts were let for the remainder of the SUR. The No. 1

Contract was for the approximately 12 mile section from Stafford Junction, Wellington to the Shropshire Union canal bridge at Gnosall (inclusive), but excluding the stations at Donnington and Hadley. This contract was awarded on 31st August, 1847 to the partnership of James Howe and Henry Jones of Great Homer Street, Liverpool. The sureties were George Thompson of Shipley, Yorkshire and Thomas Clarkson, of Liverpool. The total value of this contract was £79,505.

The No. 2 Contract was for the remainder of the line from Gnosall to Stafford, but also included the branch from Gnosall to Norton Bridge and Shallowford, which was never built. This contract was awarded to Francis Wythes, of Poole, Dorset on 4th September, 1847 in the sum of £111,153 10s. 0d. He had just completed a contract on the Southampton & Dorchester Railway, and was evidently sufficiently well known as not to need an independent surety. However, a supplement was issued to the original contract shortly after, on 24th September, 1847 specifying the individual amounts for the main line from Stafford to Gnosall (£49,662 5s. 0d.) and the branch to Norton Bridge and Shallowford (£61,491 5s 0d.). It was evidently becoming clear that the branch would not be required.

The tender of John Cobb of Newport was accepted for the building of a 'first class' station and associated works at Newport, totalling £2,142 1s. 9d. at a meeting of the Committee of Works at the SUR&CC offices in Westminster on 17th November, 1848 and the contract was subsequently issued. At the same meeting tenders were examined for the stations at Gnosall and Haughton, but it was decided not to proceed with brick buildings. Instead, further tenders were to be sought for wooden buildings, as eventually built. Evidently, as the project was nearing completion, economy was becoming the watchword, although this may also have been the thrifty influence of the LNWR.

However, at the same meeting, tenders of £110 each were also accepted for two cottages to be built, one for each of the level crossing keepers at Trench and Derrington. The cottages consisted of two bedrooms, kitchen/pantry, brewhouse and privy (both presumably out of doors), and a fixed boiler.

Whether or not to build a station at Admaston had still not been decided by the Joint Line Committee, and at its meeting on 17th October, 1848 a decision on 'the propriety of a roadside station at Admaston' was further deferred.

On 31st May, 1849 a contract for the construction of 'second class' stations and works at Donnington and Hadley was awarded to John Peplow of Oakengates (along with the sureties of Andrew Peplow, also of Oakengates and James Ward of Hadley). Peplow's tender for work was accepted, as follows:

	Donnington			Hadley		
	£	s.	d.	£	s.	d.
Offices	610	3	11	274	10	3
Platforms	112	19	9	132	4	0
Fencing	44	11	8	34	17	7
	767	15	4	441	11	10

Total value: £1,209 7s. 2d.

On 22nd August, 1849 a contract for goods warehouses, offices and stables at Shrewsbury (Abbey Foregate) and Newport was awarded to John Millington of Ketley. His surety was John Horton of Priors Lee Hall, Shifnal. The contract was for works at Shrewsbury valued at £2,542 19s. 7d., and at Newport of £570.

A final contract was issued by the SUR on 24th May, 1854 even though by this time the SUR&CC was being effectively run by the LNWR via their joint management committee. It is odd that a contract was issued at this late date by the SUR, not least because it was for the building of the Queen Street goods depot in Wellington, which was always known as the 'LNWR Goods'. The contract included the goods depot, offices, approaches, four cattle pens and 1,056 yards of sidings. The total was £2,453 15s. 7d., and the contractor was once again John Millington of Ketley, but this time his sureties were William West of Ketley, and Charles Bennion of Hill Farm, Shifnal.

The only major feat of construction on the Stafford-Shrewsbury line was the bridge at Preston Boats (later better known as Belvidere bridge) over the River Severn, just under two miles from Shrewsbury station. This was designed by William Baker, who as Resident Engineer on the S&BR designed all the major structures and stations for the S&BR and the joint line. The bridge is a typical example of Victorian elegance, consisting of two arches, each of 101 ft-span and cast by the Coalbrookdale Company, which rested on stone abutments. During the construction of this bridge two men fell into the River Severn and were drowned. Only one other fatality is recorded during the construction of the line: the cutting at the approach to Abbey Foregate in Shrewsbury partially collapsed, burying and killing one workman. As readers may well be aware, the workforce involved in railway construction were often an unruly crowd, and especially so after a few drinks. So it is not surprising that it was reported with alarm in the *Wellington Journal* of the time that rival gangs of men had fought in the streets of Wellington during February 1848.

The remainder of the work was fairly straightforward as there were no significant gradients required, the land especially from Stafford to Wellington being fairly level. However, one lengthy cutting was required west of Haughton of approximately 1½ miles through sandstone, during which 300,000 cubic yards of spoil were removed. A little further westwards, at the approach to Gnosall, the line passed over the flood plain of the Doley Brook. Although only nominally a 'brook', its flood plain is some quarter of a mile wide at this point, and was particularly marshy. This was not made any easier by persistent rain during the autumn and winter of 1848, such that an extra 260,000 cubic yards of 'ballast' were necessary over that originally estimated. West of the crossing of the SUR&CC canal at Gnosall, a tunnel of some 55 yards in length had originally been specified. However, at a meeting of the Committee of Works on 5th May,1848 it was agreed that 'materials being wanted for embankments, it has been determined by the engineer to make an open cutting'. The materials referred to are undoubtedly for the embankment at Doley Brook. Many of the materials used in the construction of the line, including rails, arrived via the canal network, and were unloaded at Gnosall on the Shropshire Union Canal 'main line', and at Lubstree wharf on the Humber Arm.

Viaduct over the River Severn at Shrewsbury as depicted in the *Shrewsbury Chronicle*, 8th June, 1849.   *Courtesy Shropshire Records & Research Centre*

Cast-iron bridge over the River Severn at Preston Boats as depicted in the *Shrewsbury Chronicle*, 8th June, 1849.   *Courtesy Shropshire Records & Research Centre*

Even though delays resulted, the line was still constructed to schedule. By contrast, the S&BR experienced considerable delays because of the bad weather on its section from Wellington to Wolverhampton, most particularly with the construction of the 471 yds-long Oakengates tunnel and the Shifnal embankment.

The 'first experimental trip' on the line was due to take place on 1st March, 1849, but was delayed and eventually occurred on 14th March, 1849 using 'an engine, tender and one carriage from the LNWR', conveying Mr Baker, plus Messrs Donaldson, Hutton and Winstanley (Resident Engineers), and the contractors Wythes, Murray, Howe and Jones. It left Stafford at noon, calling at Gnosall, Newport (at 1.00 pm) and Wellington, arriving in Shrewsbury for a late lunch. The train returned at 4.30 pm, arriving in Stafford at 6.00 pm.

The SUR line from Stafford to Wellington eventually cost £500,000 to build, and had employed some 3,300 men and 280 horses in the period of construction.

Government inspector Captain Simmonds visited the line on 2nd May, 1849, and for his formal inspection was accompanied by Robert S. Skey (SUR&CC General Manager), Henry Tootal (on behalf of the Directors), and the contractors McLeod, Murray, Howe and Jones. At the conclusion of this inspection, a dinner was consumed by the party at The Bull's Head in Wellington. Captain Simmonds (who later rose to become Field Marshal Sir J. Lintorn A. Simmonds) sent a favourable report to the Commissioner of Railways, and the official opening was scheduled for 1st June, 1849.

The *Stafford Advertiser* of 9th June, 1849 reported that the line opened 'without ceremony'. However, at the other end of the line, matters were vastly different, for the *Shrewsbury Chronicle* of 8th June, 1849 reported:

> The scene in and around the station (Shrewsbury) is very animated; gay flags and banners placed at different points along the station walls, and on the fine viaduct over the Severn were fluttering in the sunshine of as lovely a day as the heart of a tourist could wish for; the enlivening strains of a brass band lent an additional charm to a scene which received the finishing touch of interest from the varied study presented by the eager throng of pleasure makers.

At Wellington, it was reported that shops had closed for the day, as everyone was taking a holiday. Vast crowds were found at every vantage point. The *Shrewsbury Chronicle* also reported that,

> . . . at Newport, the inhabitants of all ranks had met in considerable numbers in the neighbourhood of the station, and evidently were agreeably excited by the opening of a new line of railway . . . flag floated from the tower of the church, and we observed that a private residence contiguous to the railway, exhibited two large banners. The bells of the church rang out their merry notes on the interesting occasion.

However, the *Staffordshire Advertiser* was not impressed with the facilities at Gnosall station: 'We presume that the present station house at Gnosall is merely temporary. It is a paltry wooden hut, in which the clerk and a passenger would find it difficult to exchange a ticket for money without jostling each other'.

Perhaps the difference in outlook is accounted for by the relative novelty of railways in Shrewsbury, where the Shrewsbury & Chester Railway had only

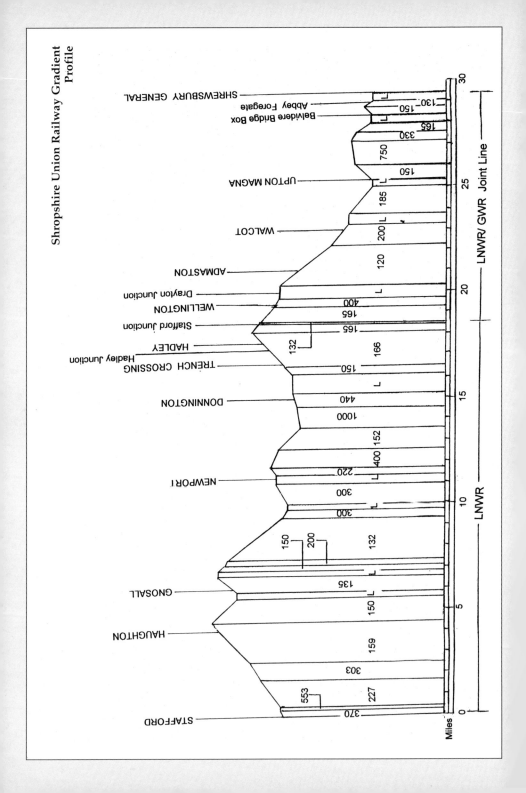

Shropshire Union Railway Gradient Profile

An early print of the original façade to Shrewsbury station, as opened in 1849, and consisting of just two storeys. The original architecture can be seen to have been beautifully balanced. Compare this view with those on pages 122, 126 and 127 when a third storey had been added. *Shropshire Records & Research*

opened (to a temporary station) on the previous 16th October. On the SUR opening day its trains also started running into the new joint station of Shrewsbury General. For Wellington and Newport, railways were something entirely new. However, at Stafford the GJR had opened its first line there some 12 years earlier.

There appears to have been one joint SUR and S&BR opening train, which divided at Wellington. The S&BR portion continued to Oakengates for lunch (which was as far as its line had opened; the remainder on to Wolverhampton not opening until 12th November of that year). The SUR train continued on to Stafford, before returning to Newport where a lunch was provided by Mr and Mrs Barlow at the Feathers Inn. Directors present on the inaugural train and at the lunch were George Holyoake, Henry Newberry, John Meeson Parsons, and Henry Tootal. A Mr Holland represented the people of Newport, and took the chair at the lunch, proposing toasts to 'The Queen', 'Prince Albert and the rest of the Royal Family', 'The Bishop and Clergy of the Diocese', 'The Earl Powis', and 'The health of the SUR&CC Chairman'. Upon the return of the SUR train to Wellington, the S&BR guests rejoined this train for the return journey to Shrewsbury. It is not recorded whether the train was formed of S&BR or LNWR locomotives and stock.

In passing, it is perhaps not entirely coincidental that the LNWR opened the Grand Junction Hotel and Railway Inn adjacent to Stafford station on 15th June, 1849. In its advertisements, it recommended the hotel 'especially for the use of customers of late trains'. As the advertisement went on to apologise for such lateness, it is probable that it was referring to the 'lateness of the hour' rather than regarding the late arrival of trains as being occasionally inevitable.

The construction and opening of the SUR has occupied a period of time in which the management of the SUR changed hands. We had earlier left the LNWR carefully watching the SUR as it started to build its line in 1846. At this time, although the SUR&CC wanted to proceed as fast as possible with the construction of its railway, it was severely restricted as to the amount of cash available. The debt resulting from its protracted completion of the Birmingham and Liverpool Junction Canal was extremely onerous, and servicing this debt had done much to erode its working capital, even though the issued share capital of the new SUR&CC company was £3.3 million. As a result, the LNWR offered the SUR&CC a perpetual lease of its railway and canal businesses in the Autumn of 1846. The terms of the lease were extremely attractive to the Directors, as the LNWR offered interest of 4 per cent on the canal issued stock until the SUR line was built, and then half of the LNWR ordinary dividends for both canal stock and SUR&CC railway shares issued to build the line. This form of guaranteed income was accepted by the SUR&CC Board, and an authorising Act (Acts 10 & 11, Vict. Chapter 121) passed in June 1847. Having obtained this foothold, the LNWR then proceeded to convince the SUR&CC to abandon its other railway projects in return for the LNWR taking over its canal interests and the debts arising from these.

In the meantime, the SUR had also deposited plans on 30th November, 1846 for a line from Shrewsbury to Worcester, with branches to Coalbrookdale, Madeley, Kidderminster and joining the OWWR at Worcester. It is very doubtful whether the SUR&CC could ever have afforded to proceed with this line as well as the others planned, but it formed part of a useful bargaining tool in discussions with the LNWR. Eventually, the SUR&CC Directors agreed and the terms of the lease were amended from June, 1849. However, these revisions had not been ratified by Parliament and were therefore legally invalid, although not illegal. Eventually, a further Act was passed, on 24th July, 1854 which formalised the amendments, although Parliament did not actually confirm these arrangements until 25th March, 1857. This meant that the SUR&CC actually remained an independent company, although all of its trading interests were performed by the LNWR, via a joint management board. This independence finally came to an end when the SUR&CC was vested in the LMSR as from 1st January, 1923 by virtue of the London, Midland & Scottish Railway (Shropshire Union Railways and Canal Company) Preliminary Absorption Scheme of 29th December, 1922.

One of the effects of the lease by the LNWR was that the SUR&CC head office in London, located at 9 Great George Street, Westminster was closed as from 26th February, 1849. Similarly, the recently opened offices in Wolverhampton were closed form the same date. All business was henceforth handled from its Chester offices, which became the head office.

Chapter Four

Early Days

As mentioned earlier the SUR/S&BR Joint Line Committee was responsible for determining on matters of operational conflict. However, the success of this committee in amicably resolving traffic disputes can only be judged in the light of subsequent events.

In the 1847 Act authorising the lease of the SUR&CC, the LNWR was bound to pool traffic on the joint line from Shrewsbury to Wellington, and not to compete for traffic, both passenger and goods. This naturally put the LNWR at a disadvantage, because the distance from Shrewsbury to Wolverhampton via the S&BR was 29½ miles, whereas the LNWR via Stafford was 46 miles. As we have seen the amendments to the 1847 Act rendered it invalid. So Mark Huish (General Manager of the LNWR) reasoned that the LNWR had no legal power to make this agreement on traffic pooling and fares, and almost from the opening began a fares war with the S&BR. As a result, the latter went to litigation in an effort to enforce the agreement, and won. However, the LNWR successfully appealed. In 1851, the S&BR tried again, and won again, but its efforts to obtain an injunction to enforce the judgement were unsuccessful. The fares war carried on, and in 1853, the S&BR again sought a further appeal, which was turned down. That seems to have been the final shot fired in the fares war, as the S&BR was taken over by the GWR with effect from 1st September, 1854 by an Act dated 7th August, 1854.

Nonetheless, the LNWR was still able to claim that its line offered the only line from Shrewsbury to London 'without break of gauge or change of carriages' until 1866. Whilst perfectly true, such a journey was still rather lengthy for third class passengers, taking up to seven hours. However, passengers to Wolverhampton had benefited, as the LNWR first class fare was still only 1s. 0d., with second class 9d., and third class just 6d. for the 46 miles, compared to fares through to Birmingham of 4s. 0d., 3s. 3d. and 2s. 6d. for the 59 miles, as from 27th January, 1851.

The initial service comprised three weekday services in each direction, leaving Stafford at 8.30 am, 2.15 and 8.45 pm, and arriving in Shrewsbury at 10.15 am, 3.50 and 10.30 pm. Trains in the up direction left Shrewsbury at 6.00 am, 12.10 and 5.00 pm, arriving at Stafford at 7.35 am, 1.45 and 6.45 pm. The first and last services stopped at all stations, whereas the middle service omitted stops at Hadley and Haughton. Admaston station first appeared in the timetables from March 1851, but oddly, there were no trains booked to stop there until September of that year. Trench station did not open until 1st January, 1855. On Sundays, there were two trains in each direction, leaving Stafford at 8.30 am and 7.00 pm, arriving in Shrewsbury at 10.15 am and 8.45 pm. In the reverse direction, the departure and arrival times were absolutely coincidental, with trains crossing at Donnington. Third class passengers were conveyed in the last down and first up services on both weekdays and Sundays.

The southern approaches to Shrewsbury in 1875. The original bridge over the River Severn contained only three running lines, and the platforms did not extend on to the bridge. Note the two small signal boxes, and the 'Abbey Curve' in the background, opened in 1867 to complete the triangle of running lines. The numerous four-wheeled carriages, and slotted post signals complete this period scene.

Shropshire Records & Research

An unfortunate, but by now quite well known accident occurred on 29th July, 1852. Joseph Thompson, a night fitter, had been required to make repairs to a leaky valve on LNWR locomotive No. 234 *Mazeppa* (an Allan/Trevithick 2-2-2 passenger engine), allocated to and stabled overnight at the Abbey Foregate SUR Shed. Having completed his repair overnight, he finished his shift, but actually left 10 minutes early at 5.50 am. Unfortunately, the day shift arrived 10 minutes late, at 6.10 am. In the meantime, the engine had disappeared. *Mazeppa* had been left in gear, and as steam pressure rose, as a result of the repair of the leaking valve, it gradually (and no doubt rather quietly) moved off on its own. It was just as well that such early engines had no cab, because a lineside railway worker near Belvidere was able to see that the engine was not manned, and raised the alarm. Another engine was summoned and proceeded to chase along after *Mazeppa*. However, some time must have elapsed because *Mazeppa* was able to catch up with the first up train of the day (6.00 am ex-Shrewsbury), and ran into the back of it whilst it was standing at Donnington station. One passenger was killed in the collision. The circumstances involved in this incident just emphasise the lack of telegraphic communication, basic signalling, and track safety conditions that we take for granted today. *Mazeppa* was repaired and continued in service until scrapped in 1878.

Theft of goods from railway vehicles became a problem, just as it had been for canal operators. However, sometimes the thieves went for items of more intrinsic value. For example, in March 1854 a 14-year-old youth was hauled before magistrates in Shrewsbury, accused of theft from the SUR. He had been caught stealing 40 lb. of brass fittings from a locomotive that had been standing in a siding at the SUR Shed at Abbey Foregate for a few weeks. He had apparently simply 'prised off' these fittings. The locomotive concerned was 'the ballast engine *Python*, which was LNWR No. 69 and was a Trevithick 2-4-0 goods engine, built at Crewe in 1853, so it was only about a year old.

A table of comparative locomotive mileages from 1849 to 1854 is given in *Appendix Two*. It will be seen that the passenger mileages are relatively stable over this period, and this is to be expected, as most of the passenger services are scheduled to a fixed timetable. However, the goods mileages show a considerable growth, trebling in the five year period, and indicating the relative prosperity brought to the area. The increase in 'assisting mileages' can be attributed to increasing train sizes during this period, and evidencing the need for larger locomotives.

The growth of freight traffic in the first few years meant that the SUR goods depot at Abbey Foregate in Shrewsbury, and the joint goods depot at Wellington were soon operating to capacity. As we have already seen, a new SUR goods depot was built at Wellington during 1854 . Subsequently, the LNWR deposited plans on 30th November, 1857 for the conversion of the SUR&CC canal goods depot in Shrewsbury, adjacent to its Victoria Basin in Howard Street, into a rail served goods depot. The engineers were stated as being Joseph Locke and John E. Errington. In the same year, the LNWR had acquired the Butter Market, which was built in 1835 to serve the canal wharf, and converted it into a grain store, in which capacity it served for many years. The shunting neck into the Howard Street goods depot was rather awkwardly sited adjacent to the up island platform of the General station. It turned sharply beneath Howard Street under a skew bridge, immediately fanning out in to an array of sidings, which served the three-road goods shed, plus lines to the canal wharf, and a headshunt which led back to the Butter Market.

Further improvements were made at Shrewsbury in 1867, with the opening on 1st May of the 'Abbey Curve', which is the chord line of no more than 25 chains that links the joint line from Wellington to the southbound Hereford line. This proved especially welcome for freight trains, that otherwise had to trundle through the station to Coton Hill before reversing and once more traversing the already busy station lines. It also proved useful for excursion traffic heading for or returning from the Welsh resorts and the Midlands.

New lines contributed to the build up of traffic at Shrewsbury, with the opening of the Hereford line in 1852, the LNWR Crewe line in 1858, and the Welshpool joint line in 1862. All this helped to increase traffic on the Wellington joint line, and at the level crossing in Underdale Road there was often considerable disruption to both road and rail traffic. This level crossing was also adjacent to the goods yards of the former SUR (on the up side) and the S&BR (on the down side). It seems probable that there were a number of shunting movements that also occupied the crossing from time to time. For the convenience of the railway, it seems that the crossing keepers acquired the habit of keeping the gates locked against road traffic for lengthy periods of time. Many complaints were made to the local newspapers, and to the joint committee concerning this practice. Despite assurances to the contrary, it appears that the practice continued. Pedestrians were not so inconvenienced, as there was a footbridge alongside the crossing. However, matters came to a head in early 1872, when the footbridge was badly damaged by a train, and was in such a dangerous condition that it was closed. The joint committee was finally put upon to resolve the situation for once and for all, and later that year a new subway and underpass beneath the railway was opened.

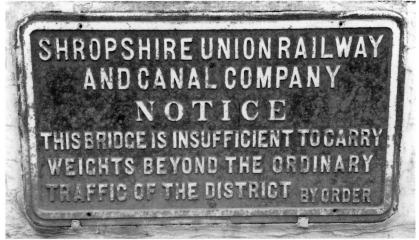

A company cast-iron board warning sign on a road overbridge, once again showing 'The Shropshire Union Railway and Canal Company'.   *Author*

Chapter Five

Prosperity and Decline of the Canals

We left the canals in 1846, when the SUR&CC was not in financial difficulties, but was suffering from a general lack of cash. However, its canal business was still very profitable, and this was recognised by its new operators, the LNWR, to provide a useful contribution to that company as well as feeding traffic on to the railway. To recap, the SUR&CC routes at this time were: Ellesmere Port via Chester to Wolverhampton, plus the branch to Middlewich; Hurleston Junction (near Nantwich) to Llangollen and the uncompleted branch towards Shrewsbury; Norbury Junction via Newport to the Shrewsbury Canal. The Montgomery Canal had always been included in the SUR&CC plans for both canal network and its railway aspirations. This was acquired in two parts. The Eastern branch (Welsh Frankton to Guilsfield) was acquired in February 1847 at a cost of £78,210, and the Western branch (Burgedin Locks to Newtown) on 5th February, 1850 at a cost of £42,000.

Meanwhile, the LNWR wished to get more traffic from the coal and ironstone mines, and ironworks and foundries in the Severn Gorge, so the LNWR leased the Shropshire Canal from 1st November, 1849 at a cost of £3,125 per annum. This canal ran from Donnington Wood via an inclined plane through Wombridge, Snedshill, and Hollinswood to Southall Bank, where the canal divided. The western arm continued to Coalbrookdale via an inclined plane, and the eastern arm continued to Blists Hill and via the now preserved Hay inclined plane to an interchange for traffic to continue on the River Severn. Much of the route of this canal lay through mining areas and so subsidence and leaks were a continuing problem. Eventually, much of the eastern arm was converted into the LNWR Coalport branch (*see Chapter Twelve*).

All of the SUR&CC canals continued to provide profits right up to the mid-1860s, and even beyond that time at least managed to cover their costs. One of the reasons may well have been that that the SUR&CC did not just obtain its income from tolls exacted on users. Unusually, the SUR&CC also maintained its own carrying fleet to operate over the whole system. This was a tradition started by the earlier Ellesmere and Chester company around 1836, and was continued by the Birmingham & Liverpool Junction company in 1842. The fleet grew rapidly and by 1870 comprised 213 narrow boats and 65 'flats'. These latter were broader boats, used on the northern section from Ellesmere Port to Chester, as well as on the Rivers Dee and Mersey. By 1889, this had reached 395 narrow boats, 101 'flats', 3 river tugs and 5 canal tugs.

The management of the LNWR showed through in that regular maintenance on the canal infrastructure was programmed, and although the LNWR has sometimes been accused of being a little too frugal in its outlook, the SUR&CC canals were in better shape than most of its rivals. In fact, the benefits of LNWR management were displayed in the £250,000 investment made by them into the development of the Ellesmere Port site for interchange of goods traffic between rail, canal and sea. Furthermore, they actively encouraged the industrial development of this area for the benefit of all concerned.

Trench incline, linking the Shrewsbury Canal at the foot, to the Wombridge Canal at the top, was abandoned from 31st August, 1921. In this 1949 view, the canal on the lower stretch can be seen to be badly infested with weed, and the incline leading to the engine house on the summit is already returning to nature. 'The Shropshire Arms' public house is on the left.
Ironbridge Gorge Museum Trust

Another 1949 view of the Shrewsbury Canal, this time at Hadley Park lock, with the Wellington to Hadley road running past in the background. Evidently this section was still in use at this time. Note the vertical lock gate.
Ironbridge Gorge Museum Trust

Never afraid to try something new, as mentioned above steam tugs were introduced on the canals, as well as on the River Dee at Ellesmere Port. Then, in 1888, an experiment in rail-hauled canal boats was tried. The venue was on the Middlewich branch just outside Crewe, where the LNWR Chester line crossed nearby, so as to facilitate the transport of the necessary equipment. Approximately one mile of 18 inch gauge track was laid on the canal bank between bridges 5 and 6. The LNWR chief mechanical engineer, Francis W. Webb, oversaw the experiment, in which the Crewe works tramway 0-4-0 locomotive *Dickie* (built at Crewe, May 1875) was used to pull the narrow boats. Whilst the experiment was successful in that it could haul up to six boats at a time, and with speeds up to seven miles per hour, there were certain practical difficulties. The main one was trying to prevent the leading boat from being pulled in towards the bank, but it was also realised that steersmen would be required on each of the boats. Furthermore, in many places the towpath changes from one side to another (for various reasons), and so expensive earthworks would be required, as well as the high cost of laying the track. In typical LNWR fashion, lessons were learnt, and no further effort was spared in this direction.

Many of the company's narrow boats were built in its own yards at Chester, Welsh Frankton, and Pontcysyllte as well as independent yards. Some steel-hulled boats were even built by the LNWR at Crewe works. Into the 20th century, the SUR&CC continued to be managed from its own offices at Chester, and not from the far flung edifice of Euston. Credit must therefore go the LNWR for realising its own limitations. This was manifested in 1921, when it was recognised that canal traffic was seriously dwindling, and so it was decided to discontinue operating the canal boat fleet. The fleet was disbanded, with

At Audlem the 'main line' faces a series of locks, two of which are seen here, adjacent to the 'Shroppie Fly' public house, converted from a former SUR&CC warehouse to provide refreshment for today's leisure cruisers.   *Author*

The SUR&CC's spiritual home had always been Ellesmere in Shropshire. The Town Arm displays some of the original company buildings, including the warehouse shown here, but considering its convenience to the town centre has not received the attention to sympathetic development that other sites have achieved.

Author

much of it going to the local firm of Fellows, Morton and Clayton, which continued to operate on the Shropshire Union (as well as other canals) until 1948.

Of the SUR&CC canal routes, the 'main line' from Ellesmere Port to Wolverhampton is still open, as is the branch from Barbridge (near Nantwich) to Middlewich. The Ellesmere route from Hurleston Junction through Whitchurch to Llangollen is also open, but the branch off this, from Welsh Frankton to Guilsfield and Carreghofa has been abandoned beyond Maesbury. Further towards Welshpool, the canal southwards to Newtown has been restored, but now carries the Montgomery Canal name once again. The branch from Norbury Junction westwards towards Telford is also derelict, apart from a short length as it passes through Newport, which has been restored purely as a recreational walkway. Further westwards, this canal joined the Shrewsbury Canal, of which two sections in Shrewsbury were closed in 1922 and 1939. The remainder was closed as part of a wartime economy measure, under the LMSR Act of 1944. On the former Shropshire Canal, a short stretch within the boundaries of Blists Hill Open Air Museum is all that remains, along with the aforementioned Hay inclined plane. Nothing remains of any of the other inclined planes in the Telford area (there were around 20 at one time), but then so much reconstruction involving changed landscape has taken place since the area was designated a New Town, that it is not surprising, if often disappointing.

Another view of the Town Arm, Ellesmere which gives holidaymakers the chance to moor within a two minute walk of the town centre.   *Author*

LONDON AND NORTH-WESTERN AND SHROPSHIRE UNION.

Week Days. Sundays.

Depart.	1 2 3	1,2	1 2 3	1,2	1,2	1,2	1 2 3	1 2	1,2
Salop	6 0	10 10	12 30				8 0	10 10	0 10 8
U. Magna	6 10		12 40				8 7		
Walcot	6 15		12 46				8 15		
Admast'n	6 20		12 50				8 20		
Wellingtn	6 25	10 30	12 55	10 28			8 25	10 28	10 28
Hadley	6 30						8 30		
Trench Cr	6 32						8 32		
Doningt'n	6 40	10 40	1 3				8 40	10 12	
Newport	6 45	10 50	1 10				8 45	10 27	
Cnosal	6 51	11 0	1 23				8 51	10 46	
Haughton	7 5						8 5	10 52	
Stafford	7 15	11 35	1 55				8 50	11 5	20 11 7
W'hampt	8 40	11 55	2 20				9 0	12 50	2 6
Birmingh	9 25	12 40	2 55				9 15	1 35	2 31
London A	1 30	3 45	6 15				6 50	5 0	5 50

Week Days. Sundays.

Depart.	1 2 3	1,2	1 2	1,2	1,2	1,2	1 2 3	1 2 8	1 2
London		6 15		12 0				10 0	
Birmingh	6 0	8 45	11 30	1 30		0 5		12 45	10 30
Wolv'rhm	6 48	9 22	11 50	2 25		0 7	20	1 30	10 50
Stafford	8 0	10 0	12 30	3 0		0 35	7	1	2 18
Haughton	8 7			3 0		0 29	8 20		
Cnosal	8 18	10 12	12 42	3 12		0 35	8 58	8 40	
Newport	8 23	10 25	12 55	3 24		8 45	9	5 2 33	
Doningt'n	8 33	10 34	1 6	8 20		9 52	13	5 17	
Trench Cr	8 38	10 30				9 50		9 16 7	
Hadley	8 42	10 43			7			9 18 7	
Wellingtn	8 47	10 47	1 15	8 40 7		5 0	23 2 46	35 7 50 2 45	
Admast'n	8 53	10 50	1 20		7		9 0	9 39 7	
Walcot	8 58	10 58	1 25	3 48 7	15			9 43 7 50	
U. Magna	9 0	11 2	1 32		7	23		9 49 8 6	
Salop A	9 13	11 12	1 40	4 0 7		35 9 40 3		10 0 8 15	

WELLINGTON AND COALPORT.

DOWN TRAINS		1,2	1 2 3	1,2	1 2 3	1,2	Sundays	
Wellington ....dep.	10 45	1 15	6 35	8 25				
Hadley	10 50	1 20	6 40	8 30				
Oakengates	11 1	1 31	6 51	8 31				
Malinslee	11 7	1 37	6 57	8 37				
Stirchley (for Dawl'y)	11 12	1 40	2 8	8 42				
Madeley Market	11 18	1 46	7 8	8 48				
Coalport ....arr.	11 25	1 58	6 18	8 55				

UP TRAINS.		1,2	1 2 3	1,2	1 2	1 2 3	Sundays	
Coalport .....dep.	8 0	12 10	4 30	6 25				
Madeley Market	8 8	12 18	4 38	6 33				
Stirchley (for Dawly)	8 15	12 25	4 45	6 40				
Malinslee	8 20	12 30	4 50	6 45				
Oakengates	8 27	12 37	4 57	6 52				
Hadley	8 33	12 43	5 6	6 57				
Wellington .....arr.	8 40	12 50	5 10	7 5				

All Trains in the above table are 1st, 2nd, and 3rd class.

The public timetable for January 1863 for the Shropshire Union Railway and the Coalport branch as published in the *Wellington Journal*, 9th January, 1863.

Chapter Six

One Hundred Years of Operation

As we have seen, the first services comprised three trains in each direction on weekdays and two on Sundays. By the Summer of 1850, the frequency had increased to four in each direction on weekdays, all of which were timed to connect at Stafford with London services, and by the mid-1850s some through carriages were introduced. By the late 1860s there were through services to Euston from Shrewsbury as follows: departing 10.20 am (arriving Euston 3.45 pm), 1.00 pm (7.30 pm), and 5.00 pm (9.30 pm). In the reverse direction, services from Euston were at 6.30 am (arriving Shrewsbury 1.15 pm), 10.00 am (3.30 pm), and 12 noon (7.25 pm). All these services conveyed first and second class passengers only. However, there were additionally four local services in each direction on weekdays. On Sundays, there were three local services in each direction, but no through trains to London.

By comparison, the GWR started running its fast trains from Shrewsbury to London in 1855, connecting with the broad gauge in Birmingham. The timings were: depart Shrewsbury 6.30 am (arrive Paddington 11.25 am), 10.25 am (3.05 pm), and 5.50 pm (10.30 pm). All of these travelled via Oxford, and conveyed first, second and third class passengers. So the best timings by the LNWR were 4½ hours, compared to the GWR's best of 4 hours and 40 minutes. However, by 1866 the GWR had introduced standard gauge through trains over the entire route, departing Shrewsbury at 10.05 am ('Parliamentary' train, arriving Paddington at 6.50 pm!), 10.45 am (3.50 pm), and 1.40 pm (6.50 pm). In the reverse direction, these were 8.00 am (12.40 pm), 10.00 am (2.37 pm), and 12 noon (5.18 pm). As the best timing was now 4 hours and 37 minutes, this hardly represented an improvement, and the situation remained much the same until the building of the Bicester cut-off, which after 1910 gave a fastest time of just under three hours.

LNWR fares from Shrewsbury to London at the opening in 1849 were £1 15s. 0d. (1st class), and £1 0s. 0d. (2nd class). By the 1870s the fares were £1 17s. 4d. (1st class), £1 6s. 0d. (2nd class) and 12s. 11d. (3rd class or 'Parliamentary'). Second class was abolished by the LNWR in 1911.

In 1880 the LNWR still had three weekday through services from Shrewsbury to Euston, with improved timings as follows: 10.20 am (arrive 3.15 pm), 12.45 pm (4.55 pm), and 10.08 pm (4.30 am). In the down direction they were at 5.15 am (9.53 am), 4.00 pm (8.00 pm), and 9.15 pm (3.00 am). The last one in each direction were mail trains, which accounts for the strange hours, and the lengthy journey times. On Sundays there was one up train at 10.08 am (5.30 pm) and two down at 10.09 am (3.35 pm) and 9.00 pm (3.00 am), the latter being a mail train. By 1910, the LNWR had four through trains in each direction (actually through carriages, rather than complete trains) on weekdays, and apart from the years of World War I, this pattern remained through to the Grouping of 1923. The LMSR discontinued through carriages for Shrewsbury just after the end of World War II, relying on connecting services of a fast and semi-fast nature.

Above: Excursions advertised in the *Wellington Journal* on 1st May, 1863.

Right: Excursions advertised in the *Wellington Journal* on 15th May, 1863.

Nonetheless, there were some through carriages conveyed over the SUR, even if these were not for Shrewsbury only. This dates back to the joint opening by the LNWR and GWR of the Shrewsbury to Welshpool line in 1862. Obviously, Euston wished to be able to offer through services to Mid-Wales and parts of the North Wales coast not connected directly to its Holyhead main line (opened throughout in 1848). In addition, in 1867 the LNWR finally penetrated the South Wales coast at Swansea, even though its main aim was the lucrative coal traffic. To reach Swansea, the LNWR had its joint line with the GWR from Shrewsbury to Hereford, but branching off at Craven Arms was its own line to Llandovery, then via joint lines and running powers over the GWR to Pontardulais and finally on its own tracks into Swansea. Most of the through services so offered were only scheduled for the Summer months, and then mostly only on Saturdays, so as to cater for the holiday traffic. Obviously, through passenger traffic, especially from Swansea via this rather tortuous route, was rather limited on weekdays. These services also showed a surprising amount of co-operation with the GWR. For example in 1904, the Summer-only 9.30 am Euston to Aberystwyth combined at Welshpool with the 9.30 am from Paddington. This latter service, incidentally, did not stop at Shrewsbury, taking the Abbey Curve instead. From the late 1920s, the LMS express 'The Welshman' (10.35 am ex- Euston) slipped a coach at Stafford, which after being attached to the next Shrewsbury train, ran regularly throughout to Swansea.

Returning to the local services, by 1880 the frequency had increased from the four of the 1860s to five each way on weekdays, with an average journey time of around one hour. In 1889 the service had expanded to nine trains each way, of which five went through to Welshpool, including two through carriages from London. By 1910 of the 12 local services between Stafford and Wellington, three had limited stops, whilst an extra five LNWR stopping services ran between Wellington and Shrewsbury (three on Sundays). Only three trains now ran through to Welshpool. By 1933, although the frequency of Shrewsbury-Stafford trains remained the same, all were now stopping trains. The GWR route prevailed as the 'fast' service, and so no stopping trains were operated solely between Wellington and Shrewsbury. This pattern continued up until the outbreak of World War II, except that through Welshpool trains further reduced to two each weekday.

After Nationalisation, the pattern of services changed yet again. On the SUR Stafford-Wellington section there were a maximum of 11 up weekday trains and 10 down weekday trains. Of the up services all except one stopped at all stations on this section, but two were non-stop from Shrewsbury to Wellington, one was from Newport to Stafford only, and one was from Wellington to Newport, whilst one of the services was Shrewsbury to Stafford stopping only at Wellington. Of the down services, all except one stopped at all stations on this section, but one was non-stop from Wellington to Shrewsbury, whilst another was semi-fast on this section, and one of the trains operated from Newport to Wellington only. One 'Mondays excepted' service ran non-stop from Stafford to Shrewsbury. The services dating from 1954 show a slight variation on this pattern, as such variations did occur during this period. In addition, there were several unadvertised trains serving Donnington, for civilian workers at the

London, Stafford, Wellington, Shrewsbury, Crewe, Chester, &c. L. & N.W.R.

London	9 15	...	5 15	7 30	9 0	..	12 30	3 0	4 0	5 15	9 0	...	10 0	...
Stafford	2 13	7 50	8 55	1055	1245	3†15	3 50	6 55	7 19	8 53	2 13	8 30	2 10	...
Newport ...	2 32	8 16	9 17	1118	1 7	3 45	4 14	7 20	...	9 15	2 32	9 0	2 40	...
Donington	...	8 24	...	1127	1 15	3 55	4 24	7 30	...	9 23	...	9 10	2 50	...
Trench	...	8 29	...	Thu	...	4 1	..	7 35	...	...	...	9 16	2 56	...
Hadley	...	8 33	...	1134	...	4 5	4 30	...	...	...	...	9 21	3 1	...
Wellington.	2 45	8 39	9 35	1140	1 27	4 12	4 36	7 42	...	9 32	2 45	9 29	3 6	...
Shrewsbury	3 0	9 7	9 53	12 21	1 50	4 35	5 0	8 0	8 0	9 55	3 0	10 0	3 35	
„ dep.	7 35	9 12	10 0	1130	1210	2 30	5 35	8 5	...	1020	1 5	10-8	...	
Hadnal ...	7 45	...		...	1219	Sat	5 45	3 15	...	...	1 15	...	...	
Yorton ...	7 51	9 25	...	1225	2 46	5 53	8 21	...	...	1 21	...	...		
Wem	8 4	9 33	1020	1150	1235	2 54	6 2	8 30	...	1040	1 31	...	...	
Prees	8 12	9 42	...	1243	3 4	6 10	8 37	...	...	1 38	...	..		
W'tchurch	8 23	9 53	1033	12 3	1256	3 15	6 20	8 46	...	1055	1 48	...	...	
Crewe arr	9 2	1030	...	1235	1 28	3 50	7 0	9 18	...	1125	2 24	1257	...	
Whitchurch	7 35	8 30	1035	...	1 5	3 25	6 30	8 52	...	...	1 48	...		
Malpas	7 47	8 41	1046	...	1 15	3 36	6 42	9 6	...	...	...	...		
Broxton......	7 55	8 48	1053	...	1 21	3 43	6 49	9 15	...	...	...	...		
Tattenhall..	8 2	8 54	...	...	1 26	3 49	6 56	9 21	...	...	...	...		
Chester	8 25	9 15	1115	...	1 45	4 10	7 15	9 43	...	2 25	3 40			
Liverpool	9 30	1030	...	...	3 15	5 5	8 20	1230	...	...	...	...		
Holyhead...	1 30	1 30	1 50	...	5 0	10 0	1130	1 0	...	5 0	9 35	...	...	

London, Stafford, Wellington, Shrewsbury, Crewe, Chester, &c. L. & N.W.R.

Holyhead ...	5 15	...	7 50	...	...	1140	12 5	3 0	3 15	...	...	5 45	...	...	
Liverpool ...	7 30	9 15	12 0	...	...	2 0	2 45	4 15	6 50	...	...	9 30	...	...	
Chester	8 50	11 0	1235	...	...	2 25	4 23	5 33	8 30	...	...	9 40	...	...	
Tattenhall..	9 4	1114	1252	...	...	2 42	...	5 46	8 45	...	...				
Broxton......	9 10	1120	1258	...	...	2 48	4 29	5 51	8 51	...	...				
Malpas	9 19	1129	1 7	...	...	2 57	4 47	5 59	9 0	...	...				
W'church arr	9 31	1141	1 20	...	...	3 10	4 59	11 9	12	...	...				
Crewe dep	8 40	...	11 5	...	...	1 7	3 15	4 30	5 40	6 55	8 35	1255	...	1130	
W'tchurch	9 16	9 33	1145	...	...	1 35	3 55	5 3	6 18	7 26	9 16	...	12 6		
Prees		...	1155	...	...		4 5	...	6 29		9 26	...	1216		
Wem	9 36	9 49	12 4	...	...	..	4 14	..	6 38		9 34	...	1224		
Yorton ...	9 44	...	1212	...	...		4 22	...	6 47	...	...		1232		
Hadnall...	...	10 0	1217	...	...		4 27	...	6 54	...	...		1237		
Salop arr	10 0	1013	1230	...	...	2 3	4 40	5 30	7 12	...	9 58	3 0	...	1250	
„ dep	7 45	9†40	1020	12 5	1245	1250	2 30	5 35	...	8 15	10 8	1030	4 25	10 8	
Wellington.	8 10	10 2	1038	1232	1 0	1 8	2 48	5 54	...	8 40	1028	11 14	53	1028	
Hadley	8 14	10 6	...	...	...		2 52	...	8 45	...	11 54	57	...		
Trench	8 17	10 9	...	...	...		2 55	...	8 48	...	11 8	5 0	...		
Donington..	8 22	1015	1047	...	1 17	3 0	6 3	...	8 53	...	1114	5 5	...		
Newport ...	8 31	1025	1054	...	1 25	3 9	6 10	...	9 3	1044	1124	5 15	1044		
Stafford......	8 58	11 0	1120	...	1 35	1 50	3 37	6 35	...	9 35	11 4	12 05	45	11 4	
London	1250	3 15	3 15	...	4 55	5 30	7 10	1020	...	...	4 30	4 30	9 30	5 30	

Public timetable for September 1880 which appeared in the *Wellington Journal* on 11th September, 1880.

An unidentified LNWR Ramsbottom 'Problem' class 2-2-2 heads out of Shrewsbury with a Stafford train composed of six-wheel carriages, with a 26 ft brake being the leading vehicle. It is seen in the cutting near Sparrow Lane on an unknown date.   *LNWR Society*

A Stafford train enters Newport station around 1910, hauled by a Bowen-Cooke 'George the Fifth' class 4-4-0. The variety of platform canopies on the down platform indicate successive additions over the years.

Shropshire Records & Research

A new culvert was laid in concrete troughs beneath the running lines at Wellington some time in the 1920-21 period. This shows work in progress in the brick-lined cutting between Church Street and Bridge Road, with an LNWR Webb '17 in. Goods' 0-6-0 in attendance.

Author's Collection

Ex-LNWR 0-8-0 No. 8945 trundles through Wellington station on 3rd August, 1935 with a Stafford-Shrewsbury mixed goods train.This locomotive was originally built in 1903 as class 'B' four-cylinder compound, being rebuilt as a class 'G1' two-cylinder simple in 1927, and class 'G2a' in 1940.

H.F. Wheeller

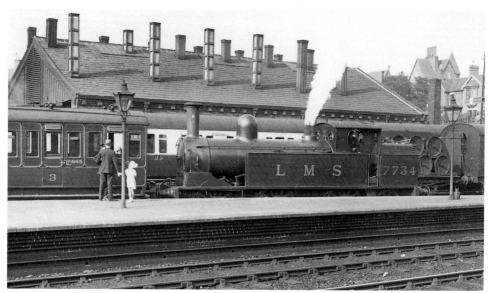

Ex-LNWR 0-6-2T Webb 'Coal Tank' No. 7734 stands in the platform at Wellington prior to departure with a local train, 3rd August, 1935. Wellington Shed can be seen in the background.
H.F. Wheeller

Webb 0-6-2 'Coal Tank' LMS No. 7787 stands in the main up platform at Wellington station in August 1936 with a train for Stafford. The vehicle next to the locomotive is an LNWR arc roof brake in LMS livery. This print was reproduced from a 'magic lantern' slide.   *LNWR Society*

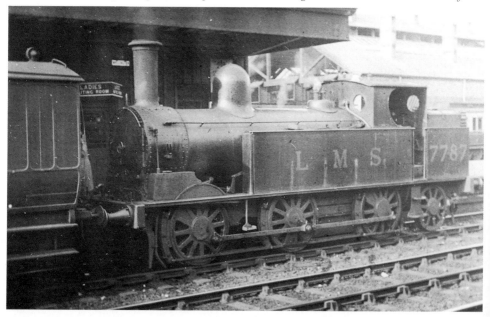

Ex-LNWR 'Prince of Wales Tank' 4-6-2 No. 6993 gets the 'Right Away' from Wellington with a Stafford train, 3rd August, 1935. *H.F. Wheeller*

Ex-LNWR 'Prince of Wales' class 4-6-0 No. 25845 waits at Wellington before departure with a passenger train for Shrewsbury on 3rd August, 1935. This was one of five locomotives of this inside-cylinder class to be unusually fitted with outside Walschaerts valve gear. These five locomotives were often known as 'Tishy' after a famous racehorse of the time, which had a habit of crossing its legs. *H.F. Wheeller*

One of William Dean's ex-GWR engines looks on as unnamed LMS 4-6-0 'Patriot' class No. 5508 arrives at Wellington with a train for Stafford, 3rd August, 1935.   *H.F. Wheeller*

Former LNWR Bowen-Cooke 'G2' class 0-8-0 No. 49410 makes a fine sight as it hauls a freight for Stafford on the up through line at Wellington around 1962.   *A.J.B. Dodd*

Army Depot. On Sundays there were two stopping trains and one 'semi-fast' service in each direction.

By 1959, and into the 1960s, the service settled on eight down weekday trains (six to Shrewsbury and two to Wellington), stopping at all stations, plus the early morning unadvertised workmen's train to Donnington, and the mail train. On Sundays, there were two trains, to Wellington only, neither of which stopped at Gnosall, and the last train (departing Stafford at 9.28 pm) did not stop at Hadley. The up weekday trains comprised a similar eight stopping trains (five from Shrewsbury and three from Wellington), plus an early Mondays-only from Shrewsbury (depart 4.20 am) to Donnington, which curiously was then worked forward to Stafford as empty stock. There was an additional stopping train on Fridays only from Wellington to Stafford at 4.45 pm, which did not call at Gnosall. Finally, the last passenger service of the day was a fast train from Shrewsbury at 11.25 pm, calling at Wellington only before Stafford. The two up Sunday services mirrored the down services in not stopping at Gnosall and Hadley.

In 1857 a Travelling Post Office (or Sorting Coach) was added to the overnight down Shrewsbury mail train at Tamworth, and was later extended onwards to Hereford by the use of a second coach. By 1902, these two coaches were merged to form a through Tamworth-Hereford service, but were separated again in 1914. Originally, the carriages would probably have been the 20 ft six-wheelers, and were replaced by the later 36 ft six-wheelers in 1875, although a 32 ft vehicle was used during 1887. In 1905, one of the old coaches was replaced by a 42 ft vehicle. In order to ensure continuity of operation for this essential service, a spare sorting vehicle was always stationed at Shrewsbury. However, the service was halted in 1915 ostensibly for the duration of hostilities, but in fact ceased altogether as from 28th February, 1917.

Special trains were always a feature of traffic at the Shrewsbury end of the line, to the extent that the General station was often very hard pressed to cope on the occasion of special events such as the Shrewsbury Show. Specials for the Races at Shrewsbury were slightly easier to cater for, as the racecourse was situated adjacent to Monksmoor Road, just to the east end of the SUR and S&BR goods depots, where a ticket platform, known as Abbey Foregate Platform was situated. So special trains for the races were terminated here, rather than in the General station. However, horse racing ceased in 1887, when the owner, Lord Tankerville, sold the land (for £17,000) to Shrewsbury Council. The Royal Show was held on this land in 1914, and gave rise to considerably increased traffic for this notable event, although the land was later used for building council houses.

From the opening of the line, all services had been worked by the engines and men of the LNWR, using LNWR stock. Whilst many of the locomotives used on passenger trains always tended to be those specifically intended for secondary services, there were always a number of older (and usually less successful) main line express types that had been cascaded from their top link duties, and allocated to both Stafford and Shrewsbury Sheds. It appears that the same can be said for much of the passenger carriages too. For even in the early days, those occasionally borrowed by the S&BR were said to be in a 'shocking' state, and obviously not up to its standards. Later, through services benefited from more

Wolverhampton's Oxley Shed received three ex-LNER 'O4' class 2-8-0s in September 1951. However, the loan was short-lived as within three weeks these were replaced by 'WD' 2-8-0s. In this rare shot, No. 63816 is passing through Wellington with a freight train towards Shrewsbury on 7th September, 1951.   *R.C. Riley*

Oxley-allocated ex-GWR 'ROD' class 2-8-0 No. 3031 heads a southbound freight out of Wellington on 30th August, 1952. This train would have taken the former S&BR route south.   *Brian Morrison*

Ex-LMS '2P' class 4-4-0 No. 40677 pulls away from Newport with the 5.50 pm from Shrewsbury to Stafford on 26th August, 1952.   *Brian Morrison*

Ex-GWR 'Hall' class 4-6-0 No. 5962 *Wantage Hall* powers through Gnosall with a diverted Birkenhead-Birmingham train on 18th October, 1953.   *W.A. Camwell*

'2P' class 4-4-0 No. 40419 restarts its Shrewsbury-Stafford train at Newport on 20th July, 1954.
Brian Morrison

Ex-LMS Fowler class '3MT' shunts empty carriage stock at Shrewsbury to form the next train to Stafford on 9th August, 1956. The Dana footbridge is visible above the locomotive.
Brian Morrison

Ex-LMS Fowler 2-6-4T No. 42400 waits to depart Wellington with a local train for Stafford c.1957. *Millbrook House/D. Johnson Collection*

Ex-GWR '28XX' class 2-8-0 No. 2871 passes through the joint station at Wellington with an evening up freight on 4th July, 1959. *Michael Mensing*

Ex-LMS 'Stanier 'Black Five' 4-6-0 No. 45004 heads the 3.54 pm Stafford-Shrewsbury train on 4th July, 1959. The train has just passed Wellington No. 4 signal box, the lines diverging to its right are the former GWR route to Market Drayton.   *Michael Mensing*

modern stock. After Nationalisation, non-corridor stock was unusual on the services and certainly from the 1950s onward most trains were formed of three Stanier 57 ft corridor coaches.

As the LNWR Southern Division and Northern Division met at Stafford from 1860 until 1862 when the divisions were abolished, it seems probable that engines from both divisions would have appeared on the line. This would have provided a considerable spectacle with the green liveries of the Northern Division engines contrasting with the vermilion red of the Southern Division, until they were all painted black (albeit the special LNWR 'blackberry' black) by Webb. After the early engines by Trevithick and Allan consisting of the 6 ft 2-2-2 for passenger work and the 5 ft 2-4-0 for goods work, the Ramsbottom 7 ft 6 in. 2-2-2 express locomotives may well have put in an appearance. Regular work was more likely to have been in the charge of his 'Problem' class 2-2-2, 'Samson' class 2-4-0 and 'Newton' class 2-4-0 locomotives on passenger work, along with the ubiquitous 'DX' class 0-6-0 engines on goods work. The Webb era produced another whole range of locomotives for passenger work, some of which are known to have been shedded at Shrewsbury, albeit ostensibly for express work on the 'North and West' route to Hereford. These were Webb's often controversial forays into compounding with divided drive for the high and low pressure cylinders, as featured in his 2-2-2-0 'Teutonic' and 'Experiment' classes, and the 2-2-2-2 'John Hick' and 'Greater Britain' classes. Later, his celebrated 'Precedent' conventional 2-4-0 passenger engines appeared, as well as the 17 in. Coal Engines', 'Coal Tanks', 18 in. 'Cauliflowers' and 2-4-2T 'Watford Tanks'.

Freight workings were also handled by many of the Webb, Whale and Bowen-Cooke 0-8-0 engines of both compound and simple expansion. The many classes of excellent 4-4-0 and 4-6-0 by both Whale and Bowen-Cooke handled all types of traffic, and several of the 'Prince of Wales' class 4-6-2 tanks were regular performers on the line. 'Precursor' class 4-4-0 LMS No. 25245 *Antaeus* was allocated to Stafford for many years, and 'George the Fifth' class 4-4-0 LMS No. 25348 *Coronation* (the 5,000th engine built at Crewe Works) and 'Prince of Wales' class 4-6-0 No. 25648 *Queen of the Belgians* also ended their days at Stafford. The appearance of LMS standard types was also commonplace, with just about every type designed by Fowler and Stanier appearing, with the possible exception of the Beyer Garratts. In the 1950s, Shrewsbury's Webb 'Coal Tank' No. 58904 was a regular performer on the Wellington to Newport duty in between its spell on the Coalport branch. Latterly, the most favoured engines to be assigned work from Stafford Shed on passenger duties were the Fowler 2-6-4T engines. Curiously, BR Standard types were not so commonly sighted, with only the Class '5MT' 4-6-0 on passenger turns and class '9F' 2-10-0 on freight turns being fairly regular, although at least one visit is known of a 'Britannia' 4-6-2 on a stopping train towards the end of steam. Because of the line's closeness to Crewe, many of these types appeared on running-in turns after overhaul, regardless of where they were based. The fairly easy going type of secondary passenger duties were ideal for such bedding down purposes. This was a feature that was to continue throughout the life of the line, and this variety brought a great deal of satisfaction to both engine crews and enthusiasts over the years. Lists of those engines allocated to Stafford and Shrewsbury Sheds in

A busy scene on the western approach to Wellington station on Easter Monday, 30th March, 1959. Ex-GWR 'Castle' class 4-6-0 No. 5001 *Llandovery Castle* is approaching with empty stock as Wellington-allocated BR Standard '82XXX' 2-6-2T No. 82006 departs with the 10.00 am for Market Drayton and Crewe. In the left foreground we see the cattle dock facilities and in the distance beyond the 'Castle' is Queen Street goods depot. *Michael Mensing*

A down Western Region passenger train between Wellington and Admaston headed by 4-6-0 'Castle' class No. 5047 *Earl of Dartmouth* on 4th July, 1959. *Michael Mensing*

Fowler 2-6-4T No. 42309 pulls away from Upton Magna with an up passenger train on 15th August, 1959.

Ex-LMS Stanier '8F' class 2-8-0 No. 48660 is seen blowing off while approaching Newport with an eastbound freight on 5th August, 1961.   *Michael Mensing*

Super power for the three-coach 4.01 pm to Shrewsbury train. Rebuilt 'Royal Scot' 4-6-0 No. 46166 *London Rifle Brigade* shortly after taking the SUR line from Stafford on 14th October, 1961. The mineral wagons serving the Universal Grinding Works, in the background, are stabled on the site of the original Burley Fields Siding.   *Michael Mensing*

Stanier LMS '8F' class 2-8-0 No. 48258 (with a Fowler tender) runs through Stafford station, during the rebuilding and electrification work of 1961/2, with a freight for the SUR line. The coaling plant and ash handling plant of the locomotive depot can be seen behind the locomotive.
                                                                                  A.J.B. Dodd

Fowler class '4' 2-6-4T No. 42400 has arrived from Stafford in Wellington's platform 5, the northern of the two bay platforms on the down side. There were no run-round facilities at these two bay platforms. The locomotive had to propel the coaches into a headshunt parallel to the main line, then after being released, the coaches returned to the bay platform by gravity. Occasionally, Shrewsbury trains backed out from the bay platform on to the main line before continuing their journey. *A.J.B. Dodd*

Fairburn 2-6-4T No. 42230 blows off as it waits to leave Stafford with the 5.40 pm Wellington train on 4th March, 1961. Several Fairburn tanks were released from store at Neasden Shed during the winter of 1960/61 to Midlands sheds, to deputise for inoperative dmus. Consequently, the engine retains a 14D (Neasden) shedplate on its smokebox door. *Michael Mensing*

There seems to be a good number of passengers for Stafford in this view as Fairburn 2-6-4T No. 42186 drifts into the platfrom at Newport.   *David Lawrence*

The Western Region's 2.10 pm London (Paddington) to Birkenhead (Woodside) service is hauled by diesel-hydraulic 'Warship' class No. D817 *Foxhound* and is seen just east of Wellington station on 27th August, 1962.   *Michael Mensing*

the early days, and Stafford and Wellington Sheds in 1945, 1947 and 1958 are included in *Appendix Four*.

Certainly, all passenger services were regularly steam hauled up until 1962. However, diesel multiple units were used during the last two years on the SUR line from Stafford to Wellington, but were and still are the mainstay of stopping services from Wolverhampton to Shrewsbury along the joint line.

There was considerable through working of freight traffic over the SUR throughout its life, particularly when considering its position as a feeder for traffic to and from Mid- and South Wales, and going to the West Midlands and the South. Traffic from these areas travelling northwards would be routed via Whitchurch to Crewe, and for Chester via Whitchurch or Wrexham to ease congestion on the West Coast Main Line. Originating traffic comprised coal from the Lilleshall Company (later National Coal Board) at Donnington exchange sidings, as well as other engineered products from the multiplicity of foundries and engineering works in the Wellington area. Some of these are discussed in Chapter Ten. The beet sugar works at Allscott also generated raw beet and coal traffic inwards, and refined products in vans outwards. Stone traffic was fed from the Shropshire & Montgomeryshire Railway, and timber found its way from the Mid-Wales forests for use in the construction and mining industries. Because of the nature of the countryside that the line traversed, there was also considerable agricultural traffic, necessarily of a seasonal nature, both in livestock and produce. In addition, milk churns could be seen being loaded or unloaded at most of the stations from daily passenger trains.

Wellington station saw a great deal of the freight traffic passing through, from both the SUR and S&BR. Latterly, one of the principal freight routes from the Midlands to the North and North West was from Oxley Sidings (on the northern side of Wolverhampton) to Crewe marshalling yards. This travelled over the GWR route from Wellington via Market Drayton and Nantwich. Such was the importance of this traffic, and that originating in Wales, that a proposal was made in 1961 for a new, massive marshalling yard to be constructed on the joint line near Walcot, with an east-facing junction to the Market Drayton line forming a chord to the existing line. Thus traffic from the Midlands, South Wales and West Wales could travel northwards via Crewe, avoiding Shrewsbury or through Shrewsbury. The yard was intended to be used in either direction, consisting of a group of 48 marshalling sidings, with a hump at one end and departure sidings at the other. There were to be facilities for the repair of wagons, servicing of diesel locomotives and transhipment of loads (where necessary) including road access. However, before any work could begin on this proposal, BR decided to abandon its customers who could only generate traffic by the single wagon load, and concentrate instead on the movement of bulk traffic and to develop the Bescot site. This short-sighted decision gave road hauliers an unexpected bonus, but has since thankfully been reversed as soon as BR freight traffic was privatised.

The section from Stafford to Wellington was subject to an overall speed limit of 60 mph, although there was an understandable 15 mph permanent restriction over the junction at Stafford, and a limit of 50 mph round the curve and through Newport. 'Whistle boards' were sited one mile each side of the three level crossings, at Derrington, Donnington and Trench Crossings.

Stanier 'Jubilee' 4-6-0 class No. 45578 *United Provinces* arrives at Newport with the 3.59 pm Stafford-Shrewsbury service on 5th August, 1961. The first carriage in the train appears to be of LNER origin. In the distance is the large grain silo which was served by sidings.

Michael Mensing

''Jubilee' class 4-6-0 No. 45651 *Shovell* restarts the 5.45 pm Shrewsbury-Stafford train from Admaston Halt on 27th August, 1962. By this date, passengers wishing to leave the train at Admaston were required to give prior notice to the guard. Engine crews slowed at the approach to the Halt, and if no intending passengers were visible, did not stop.   *Michael Mensing*

Stanier 'Black Five' 4-6-0 No. 45401 rolls an evening Stafford to Shrewsbury stopping train past Wellington No. 2 signal box on the left, and into the station around 1962. The headshunt used for releasing locomotives from the bay platforms can be seen on the right. *A.J.B. Dodd*

Stanier 'Jubilee' class No. 45662 *Kempenfelt* is seen just west of Hadley with the 4.01 pm Stafford-Shrewsbury train on 27th August, 1962. *Michael Mensing*

BR Standard class '5' 4-6-0 No. 73026 makes a rousing start from Donnington with a Shrewsbury-bound stopping train, around 1963/64.   *P. Ward*

Rebuilt 'Royal Scot' class 4-6-0 No. 46124 *London Scottish* stands in Wellington station around 1963/64 with the usual three coaches bound for Stafford. All Saints' church dominates the skyline.   *A.J.B. Dodd*

Stanier 'Jubilee' class 4-6-0 No. 45641 *Sandwich* rolls over the level crossing into Donnington station with a Stafford to Shrewsbury train formed of the usual three-coach set of 57 foot corridor stock in 1963-4. *R. Bannister*

An unidentified Stanier '8F' class 2-8-0 passes Wellington station on the up through line with a lengthy freight on 26th June, 1964. The 'modernised' coaling stage of Wellington MPD can be seen in the background. *E. Talbot*

Stanier 'Jubilee' class 4-6-0 No. 45681 *Aboukir* brings its Stafford-bound train to a halt in Trench Crossing station around 1963/64. The rear coach appears to be of former LNER Gresley design.
A.J.B. Dodd

BR Standard class '5' 4-6-0 No. 73026 makes a sure footed start from Trench Crossing station and over the level crossing with a stopping train, increased to four coaches, for Stafford. The level crossing gates appear to be the originals, made entirely of metal, riveted and brazed together.
A.J.B. Dodd

Stanier 'Black 5' 4-6-0 No. 45190 passing Church Aston, west of Newport, with a Stafford to Shrewsbury train in July 1964.   *P. Ward*

Stanier 'Jubilee' class 4-6-0 No. 45620 *North Borneo* is seen hauling an eastbound freight train 1½ miles east of Newport on 13th April, 1963.   *Michael Mensing*

Stanier 'Black 5' 4-6-0 No. 45190 near Gnosall with a Stafford to Shrewsbury train in 1964.
E. Talbot

A splendid view of Fowler class '4' 2-6-4T No. 42400 accelerating away from Donnington with the 7.15 am Stafford to Shrewsbury train on 29th August, 1964.   *Gerald T. Robinson*

Signalling and telegraph is a subject often overlooked, but as illustrated by the 1852 accident involving *Mazeppa*, it is of paramount importance, not only to the safe running of a railway, but also to its efficient running. At the opening of the SUR, there were no fixed signals as we know them. Instead, uniformed signalmen ('bobbies') stood at defined positions along the line and by the use of flags operated a time interval system of block occupation. After a train had passed, no further trains would be allowed past for five minutes. During the next five minutes trains would be signalled to proceed with caution, and after 10 minutes had elapsed the line would be given as clear. To indicate these conditions, the signalman would stand to attention holding a white flag vertically to indicate 'line clear'; to indicate 'proceed with caution' he would hold the white flag at 45 degrees above the horizontal; to indicate 'track defect ahead' he would hold the white flag at 45 degrees below the horizontal; and for 'stop' he would hold a red flag. Fixed semaphore signals were introduced from the mid-1850s onwards, although it is not known at which date the SUR can be said to have been fully equipped. Lower quadrant signals of GWR origin were installed on the joint line, and those of LNWR pattern on the SUR Stafford to Wellington section. On the LNWR section in later years most of the signal arms were standard LMS upper quadrant, with some BR standard upper quadrant.

The most important communications benefit for the railways was the introduction of telegraph. This was first used in this area on the S&BR in 1852 to protect trains travelling through Oakengates tunnel, as it seems that most people still had a morbid fear of tunnels, not always unreasonably held. The advantages of telegraph were immediately apparent, and it was fairly quickly introduced throughout the GWR by the mid-1850s. It is not known when block telegraph was introduced on the line, but it is believed to have been at least coincidental with that elsewhere on the GWR.

To conclude this chapter, it is appropriate to give examples of two 'incidents' that were both unfortunate, but illustrate the hazards of everyday railway life. The first incident occurred at Stafford station on the evening of 17th January, 1913 during a very thick fog. As the 5.17 pm train for Shrewsbury was pulling out of the station, it was in collision with a light engine. It is believed that the light engine was fouling the running line, rather than blocking it, as the result of the collision was relatively minor, with the only casualty being that 'one of the firemen sustained a nasty cut on the head, but after receiving first aid he was able to return to duty'. No passengers were injured, although some experienced a slight jolting. The train was delayed for about half an hour, and traffic generally on the Shropshire line was not affected by the collision. The account does not, however, mention whether the train continued with the same engine.

The second incident occurred on the morning of 2nd February, 1942. Mr J.J. Evans, station master at Gnosall reported that William Brough, aged 62, of Rose Hill Cottage, Gnosall had been knocked down and killed by a goods train near Haughton station. Brough was a ganger platelayer, a job which he had held for practically all of his working life, and for the last 39 years in the Gnosall district. The *Staffordshire Advertiser* of 7th February, 1942 continues that he was walking

The first of two further views of Fowler 2-6-4T No. 42400. Here she is seen leaving Newport with the 5.59 pm to Wellington on 27th August, 1964.   *Millbrook House/D. Johnson Collection*

This time Fowler class '4' 2-6-4T No. 42400 struggles up the 1 in 166 from Hadley to Haybridge with the 9.08 am coal train from Donnington exchange sidings to Ironbridge power station on 23rd September, 1964. Some vans are included in the consist, next to the engine, and these probably originated from the Ordnance Depot at Donnington.   *P. Ward*

A view looking down onto Admaston Halt with Stanier 'Black Five' No. 45001 arriving with the 6.03 pm to Stafford on 29th August, 1964. *Millbrook House/D. Johnson Collection*

Stanier 'Jubilee' class 4-6-0 No. 45577 *Bengal* was a regular on the line in its final days. It is seen here on 3rd September, 1964 just four days before cessation of passenger working, leaving Donnington for Shrewsbury. *P. Ward*

Something of a contrast is provided in these two views of local passenger services at Donnington in 1964. Here we see 2-car Birmingham RCW dmu (later class '104') arriving with a train to Shrewsbury on 23rd August, 1964. A closure notice is visible on the right of the photograph.

Michael Mensing

Super power for a Shrewsbury to Stafford passenger working, with BR Standard Pacific No. 70023 *Venus*, seen leaving Donnington for Stafford.   *P. Ward*

BR Standard class '5' 4-6-0 No. 73025 takes the Stafford line at Wellington (Stafford Junction) with the 7.42 am Shrewsbury-Stafford service on 29th August, 1964. *Gerald T. Robinson*

Stanier 'Black Five' 4-6-0 No. 45262 is seen ambling along ¼ mile west of Gnosall with an eastbound mixed goods train consisting only of four wagons and a brake van on 29th August, 1964. *Michael Mensing*

over his length of the line between Gnosall and Haughton. He walked along the down line towards Haughton (i.e. correctly facing any oncoming traffic), and when about 200 yards from the latter station he saw an engine and goods van approaching towards him from Stafford. He stepped out of its path into the up line, and was immediately afterwards knocked down by a goods train travelling from Shrewsbury to Stafford and instantly killed. His cap was found on the buffer of the engine, and his body had been carried for 45 yards. The guard of the down goods train said he saw a person move across the line as they approached, and thought that the noise of his train prevented Brough hearing the other train behind him. The morning was misty, with less than 30 yards visibility. It is somewhat surprising that a railwayman with so much experience should have made such a fatal error, but human nature is often unpredictable.

BR Standard class '9F' 2-10-0 No. 92077 heads the Railway Correspondence & Travel Society's 'East Midlander' railtour and is captured here near Gnosall.   *J.B. Bucknall*

Chapter Seven

Shropshire & Montgomeryshire Railway

A brief description of this railway and its history is relevant here, because during the years that it was open, it generated traffic on to the SUR. This was fed via a west-facing junction (known as Potteries Junction) on to the joint SUR/SBR line in Shrewsbury, in the cutting west of the Belvidere Road bridge and about 100 yards before the next overbridge at Sparrows Lane. Also situated at this site were the exchange sidings, which became known as the 'Potts Yard'.

From the junction, access was made along a single line leading directly on to the Shropshire & Montgomeryshire Railway (S&MR) line to Llanymynech, or via a backshunt into the S&MR Abbey station and goods yard.

The line went through an amazing sequence of owners and closures. Initially, it was constructed in 1866 by the Shrewsbury & Potteries Junction Railway, which ran the 3¼ miles to Redhill, where it made an end-on junction with the Shrewsbury & North Wales Railway, whose line continued the 14¼ miles to Llanymynech. These two companies merged on 16th July, 1866 to form the Potteries, Shrewsbury & North Wales Railway (PSNWR), before the official opening of the line on 13th August, 1866. The PSNWR had pretensions for a line north-west to Stoke, which would have required running powers over the SUR/S&BR joint line. However, the line was never built and the running powers never obtained. The PSNWR was very soon in financial trouble, and traffic ceased on 21st December, 1866, after a sale of surplus rolling stock and equipment yielded insufficient funds to continue. Services were resumed in December 1868 but at a much reduced level. Finally, a Receiver was appointed in 1877, services were suspended by the Board of Trade on 22nd June, 1880 and the company was wound up on 18th July, 1881. Earlier, the independent Stafford & Uttoxeter Railway (formed in 1862 with the support of the SUR&CC, but not the LNWR) had attempted to obtain running powers over the SUR and S&BR from Stafford to Shrewsbury in a Bill promoted in 1879. Whilst other aspects of this Bill were approved by the Parliamentary Committee on 30th April, 1879 these running powers were opposed by the LNWR and not granted. This was a blow to Shrewsbury Town Council who had petitioned for these facilities. The following year, the PSNWR attempted to interest the Great Northern Railway (GNR) which was in the process of acquiring the independent Stafford & Uttoxeter Railway. The GNR saw this as an opportunity to reach into North Wales, and promoted a Bill during 1880 requiring running powers over the SUR and S&BR from Stafford to Shrewsbury, and thence via the PSNWR to the Cambrian Railways at Llanymynech. However, the LNWR vigorously opposed the Bill, and it was dropped on 21st June, 1880. As we have seen, the effect was that the PSNWR closed the following day.

Through its rather chequered history, the S&MR did provide some interesting traffic for onward movement over the SUR/S&BR joint line, such as stone from the quarries at Criggion, and in the Llynclys area, also including lime from the Lilleshall Company's quarries at Nantmawr to go forward to their furnaces at Oakengates. In addition, the Midland Railway Carriage & Wagon Works (an independent company, with absolutely no connection to the

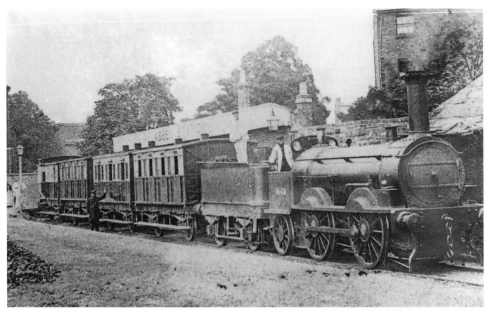

Above: Shrewsbury Abbey station in the early 1870s, with McConnell 0-4-2 No. 1859 waiting to depart with a train of ancient four-wheelers. This locomotive was built by Bury, Curtis & Kennedy in 1848 for the Southern division of the LNWR, whose running number it still carried whilst on this line. It had been acquired by the Potteries, Shrewsbury & North Wales Railway in 1872, but by 1875 it had left the line for an unknown destination.

LNWR Society

Right: Advertisement for excursion on 'The Potts' which was published in the *Wellington Journal* on 22th May, 1875.

POTTERIES, SHREWSBURY, AND NORTH WALES RAILWAY.

SHREWSBURY SHOW.

MONDAY, May 31st, 1875, EXCURSION TICKETS at Cheap Fares will be issued from Shrewsbury to BREIDDEN and LLANYMYNECH, and the undermentioned Stations, by   Special Train, leaving the Abbey Station at 1.0 p.m.

	p.m.	1st class	Cov. cars.
Leave Salop (Abbey Station)...1	0		
,, Ford 1	20	1s. 6d.	0s. 9d.
,, Shrawardine 1	25		
,, Nesoliff 1	30	2s. 0d.	1s. 0d.
,, Kinnerley 1	38		
,, Melverley.................1	49		
,, Crewe Green.............1	54		
,, Llandrinio Road 1	59	2s. 6d.	1s. 3d.
Arrive Crigglon or Breidden...2	2		
Leave Maesbrook 1	45		
Arrive Llanymynech 1	50		

Children under 12 half-price.

The Excursion Tickets will be available to return by the Trains leaving Llanymynech at 7-55 p.m., and Breidden at 7-30 p.m.

A. JUDD, General Manager.

Abbey Station, Shrewsbury,
May, 1875.

Midland Railway) was situated alongside the Hereford line, just north of the LNWR and GWR engine sheds at Coleham. This was probably the largest engineering works in Shrewsbury for most of the 19th century. Despite its location, it had no rail connection to the GWR or LNWR lines; its only rail link was a spur to the SMR, until the PSNWR was closed in 1881. This closure prompted the works to put in a new spur, this time to the joint LNWR / GWR Hereford line. Until this time, most of their output, and much of their raw materials must have been transported via the spur to Potteries Junction.

The short line linking the S&MR near Abbey station to Potteries Junction and the Potts Yard was not immune from incident, and it is not really surprising considering the disregard for proper railway procedures of the time that were evident on the PSNWR. On 16th October, 1875 an LNWR goods train was shunting in the Potts Yard, and somehow three wagons standing at the bottom end of the yard were knocked over the scotch blocks and ran down the incline towards Bell Lane (i.e. towards the Llanymynech line). Apparently, such incidents were not unusual as there were no catch points at the sidings exit. However, this time there was a mineral train coming up the grade and under the Abbey Foregate Road bridge in the opposite direction. It was formed of an 0-6-0 tank engine running bunker first, and 14 wagons. The driver saw the approaching wagons, but could do nothing other than apply his engine brake, as there was no brake van in his formation. It had long been 'common practice' on the PSNWR for braking to be applied by the brakesman leaping from wagon to wagon pulling on the individual wagon brakes. In the ensuing collision, the locomotive and the first six wagons were derailed by the impact and the driver was caught between the bunker and the firebox, subsequently dying of his injuries.

The railway lay derelict from 1880 until 19th September, 1890 when the Shropshire Railways Company took over, and immediately began to refurbish the track and stations. However, its programme of work stopped suddenly on 15th July, 1891 and on 11th November, 1891 a Receiver was appointed. The line again went to sleep, and during this time the link to the SUR/S&BR line at Potteries Junction was removed. The next owner was the Shropshire and Montgomeryshire Light Railway, promoted by the inimitable Colonel Holman F. Stephens. Another programme of reconditioning was begun, this time starting from Llanymynech, following confirmation of the Light Railway Order on 11th February, 1909. The formal opening was on 13th April, 1911 and was followed by 20 years of steady, if unspectacular, traffic.

During the 1930s traffic dwindled and services became more irregular, so that passenger services ceased on 6th November, 1933 except for occasional excursions. The system remained in a moribund state until taken over in July 1941 by the War Department, which constructed a complex of armament stores along the line. It remained in WD 'civilian' status from 1947 to 29th March, 1960 when officially closed, and handed over to British Railways which had lifted the entire line by 1962, with the exception of an additional spur added between the site of Abbey station and the former Shrewsbury to Bridgnorth line. This was used to facilitate the use of the Abbey station as an oil depot.

There is now no trace at all of Potteries Junction and the Potts Yard, and the spur is now part of a relief road. The site of Abbey station and goods yard is now a car park.

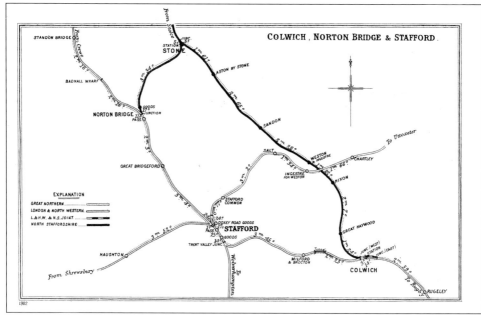

Railway Clearing House map of Stafford in 1902.

A view along the main line platforms, looking north, at Stafford on 19th September, 1959. Readers familiar with Crewe and Rugby stations will recognise the similarity of design.

H.C. Casserley

Chapter Eight

Description of the Line

The original Stafford station was opened by the Grand Junction Railway on 5th July, 1837. Little is known of this original station, which was soon found to be inadequate and did not survive for long. In 1844, a new station designed by John Cunningham of Liverpool was built, in an Elizabethan style. This station consisted primarily of two platforms, one each for up and down services.

However, once again this station and the associated track layout proved inadequate for the rapidly expanding services, which now encompassed lines to Rugby via the Trent Valley (opening 15th September, 1847), the SUR (from 1st June, 1849), as well as the North Staffordshire Railway's running powers from Stoke via Norton Bridge (17th April, 1848). Therefore, a new station was constructed by the GJR's successor, the LNWR, to the design of William Baker and built by John Parnell of Rugby, opening in 1861. This station followed more of the Gothic style favoured for most stations and public buildings of the time, and featured the typical LNWR 'train shed' also well known in the designs of Euston, Rugby and Crewe stations. This station expanded on the principle of the two platform station, but was sited slightly further north than the 1844 station, and now included a bay platform on the north side of the up platform, as well as bays at both the north and south ends of the down platform. The northern bay of the down platform was used for SUR trains. Later, the independent Stafford & Uttoxeter Railway opened (on 23rd December, 1867), and was operated by the Great Northern Railway from 11th August, 1879. From the outset, Uttoxeter trains used the northern bay of the up platform.

Traffic continued to mount, such that in the late 1880s the station was remodelled once more. The western side of the down platform was converted into a further island platform, and the bays, formerly at each end of the down platform were retained. The new island platform was furnished with a transverse ridged canopy that somehow did not seem in keeping with the remainder of the station architecture. This island platform henceforth became used by SUR trains.

The electrification of the West Coast Main Line in the 1960s required the modernisation of Stafford station, which was duly completed by December 1962. On this occasion the layout of the station platforms and running lines remained basically unchanged. However, the northern bays on the island platform were linked to the southern bays, thereby dividing the island platfrom into two. The old station buildings that were swept away in their entirety, being replaced by typical 1960s concrete and glass structures which remain to this day. Although the design is more functional than stylish, it cannot really be said to be unacceptable. Or is it the passage of time that has made it acceptable?

The SUR diverges from the LNWR West Coast Main Line just past Stafford No. 5 signal box, about a quarter of a mile north of the station. As the line swings westwards, it passes the works of W.G. Bagnall Ltd, the once famous locomotive builders, which is situated on the corner of this junction (*see Chapter Ten for description of any industrial railway systems encountered in this chapter*). Rail

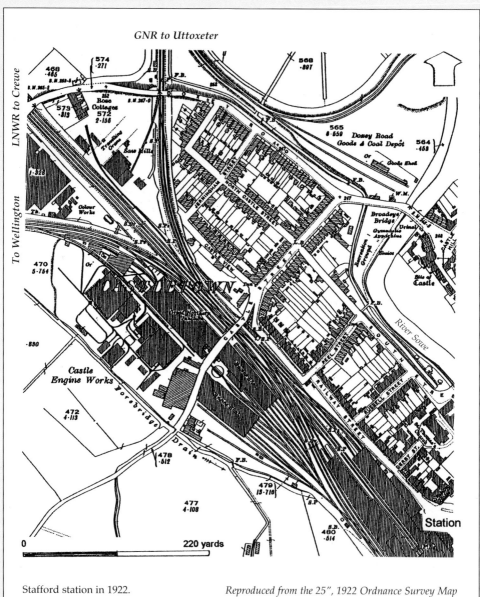

GNR to Uttoxeter

LNWR to Crewe

To Wellington

468
·445

574
·271

568
·897

573
·813

Rose
Cottages
572
2·158

565
8·559

Dozey Road
Goods & Coal Depot

564
·458

Goods Shed

Colour
Works

Broadeye
Bridge

Gymnasium

Site of
Castle

470
5·754

·830

Castle
Engine Works

River Sowe

472
4·113

Drain

478
·512

479
15·710

477
4·108

480
·514

Station

0
220 yards

Stafford station in 1922.

Reproduced from the 25", 1922 Ordnance Survey Map

The south end of Stafford station, during the LMS period, with a 'Prince of Wales' class 4-6-0 stationary in the up platform, whilst a 'Claughton' class 4-6-0 passes on the fast line with a southbound express.   *LNWR Society*

The north end of Stafford station, again during the LMS period, with three former LNWR locomotives visible. The engine in the centre road (*on the left*) is almost certainly a 'Prince of Wales' class 4-6-0 and appears to ready to transfer a through carriage to a northbound service, or has just detached it from one. The centre engine is a 'Claughton' 4-6-0 on a through northbound service, whilst the right-hand engine in the bay platform is a 'George the Fifth' class 4-4-0, probably with a connecting Shrewsbury train. The bay platform on the left was used by Great Northern trains for the Uttoxeter line.   *LNWR Society*

A general view of the north end of Stafford station. A Stanier Pacific and dmu can be seen waiting at the platforms. The carriage stock on the right will form a train for the Shropshire Union line.   *J.B. Bucknall*

Ivatt class '2MT' 2-6-0 No. 46421 is seen departing Stafford station with the 5.35 pm train to Wellington on 7th August, 1956.   *Brian Morrison*

A train from Shrewsbury has just arrived in Stafford on 5th May, 1964 behind Fowler class '4' 2-6-4T No. 42421. This locomotive and No. 42400 were transferred to Stafford Shed from Saltley in 1963, having been displaced by diesel multiple units in the Birmingham area. The catenary for the West Coast Main Line electrification scheme is now in place by this date   *E. Sabin*

English Electric type '4' 1Co-Co1 No. D341 arrives at Stafford with the 9.25 am Glasgow (Central)/9.20 am Edinburgh (Waverley) to Birmingham (New Street) on 18th August, 1963. Partially obscured by the main line catenary is the Shropshire Union line which curves away in the centre background. The line curving away to the right is the former Great Northern line to Uttoxeter.   *Michael Mensing*

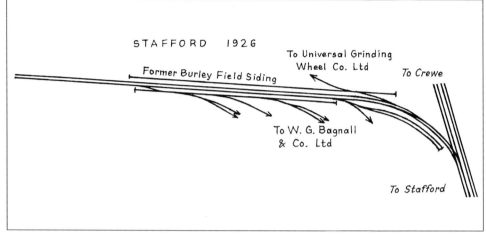

Diagram of track plan of the Shropshire Union line at Stafford in 1926.

EX-LMS Fowler '4F' 0-6-0 No. 44434 trundles off the Shropshire Union line and across the junction on to the West Coast main line at Stafford with a mixed goods train on 4th March, 1961. W.G. Bagnall's works can be seen on left. The original SUR engine shed was located on the far siding, and next to the milepost on the left   *Michael Mensing*

access into its yard was gained from the SUR down line, via a headshunt. The SUR line was now on its own, being double track throughout. On the opposite side of the line from Bagnall's works is the works of the Universal Grinding Wheel Co. Ltd, for whom a siding was also provided. This siding came off the SUR's own public siding known as Burley Field Siding, which was the nearest that the SUR came to providing independent goods facilities in Stafford. Of course, by the time the line was finished it was unnecessary to have separate goods facilities, as the LNWR was running the line and had ample goods depots and warehouses in Stafford.

The line now ran fairly straight westwards and reasonably level, entering a short, low cutting then climbing steadily at 1 in 227 across open countryside until reaching Derrington, about 1½ miles from the Stafford main line junction. No station was ever provided for this small village, despite the fact that the line passed right alongside its northern perimeter. Perhaps it was considered in the 1840s that stout countryfolk would not be interested in such a short ride into Stafford, over a distance that could easily be walked. Just at the western end of Derrington the line passed over a level crossing, distinguished by the crossing keeper's cottage (necessary for even such a minor lane) and the typical SUR crossing gates. These were unusually made of iron, riveted and bolted together, and hung from cast-iron posts. For the double track crossings, four gates and posts were required.

Still climbing, first at 1 in 303, then steepening to 1 in 159 for nearly two miles, the line continued quite straight in a south-westerly direction crossing several brooks via low bridges and an embankment of about ¾ mile in length, until about to enter the Haughton cutting. Just before the start of the cutting was Haughton station (4 miles), on a rising gradient of 1 in 159 and actually situated in the hamlet of Shut Heath, some ¾ mile from Haughton village. The main station facilities, comprising booking office, waiting room and toilets were located beneath the road overbridge on the up side, and a smaller, wooden waiting shlter was sited on the down side. A small goods yard, principally for coal, was provided on the south side of the down platform. There was no covered goods accommodation. Also on the up platform was a ground frame protected by a small cabin, mainly for operating the points into the goods yard. It was an early casualty, closing to passengers on 23rd May, 1949 and to goods on 5th August, 1957. The station was demolished very shortly afterwards.

Now the line dived at 1 in 150 into the red sandstone Haughton cutting, and very shortly afterwards passed beneath the A518 Stafford to Wellington road. As the railway curved in a more north-westerly direction, it emerged from a second, shallower cutting, and after passing beneath a farm track bridge, it ran on to an embankment lifting it over the surrounding countryside for the next mile. Firstly, the line passed over the Doley Brook, and the traveller would find it surprising that this relatively minor brook has created such a wide flood plain through Gnosall. Whilst on the curve, the line entered Gnosall station (6 miles), which seems to have been built by someone with an agricultural bias. The station buildings on each side of the line were identical, and were constructed of wood. The style had great character, and can best be described as being after the English barn style! Viewed from the end, the buildings had a semi-circular

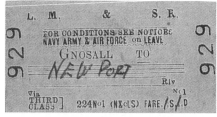

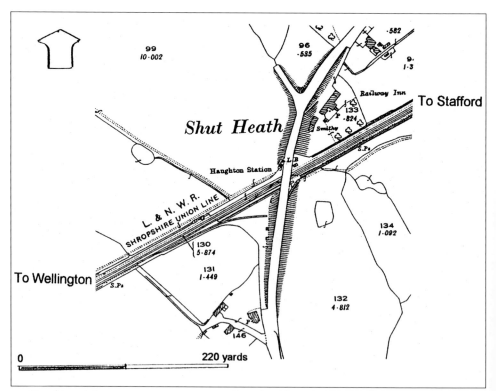

Haughton station.   *Reproduced from the 25", 1924 Ordnance Survey Map*

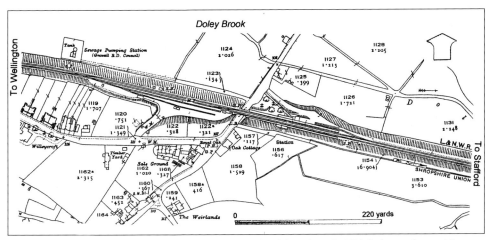

Gnosall station.

Reproduced from the 25", 1924 Ordnance Survey Map

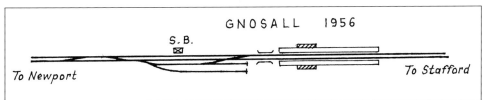

Gnosall station seen in pre-Grouping days, looking towards Stafford. The up starter signal arm and the down home are mounted on the same post, doubtless the result of LNWR parsimony, as well as the desire for clear sighting of the signals! A member of the station staff can be just discerned tending to the flower beds on the down platform, which were always a matter of considerable pride at this station, even through BR days. *E. Talbot Collection*

By early BR days the signals had been replaced by standard BR upper quadrant arms, and the up starter repositioned on the left, as seen in this view again looking towards Stafford. However, the platform lamps remained lit by oil.   *E. Talbot Collection*

Looking westwards through Gnosall station on 1st August, 1957. Gnosall signal box can be seen in the distance, which controlled access to the small goods yard. The station retained its mixed use of concrete, brick paviors and wood for the platform surfaces. The abutments for the bridge carrying the line over the Stafford to Newport line are just beyond the platform ends.
E. Talbot Collection

Gnosall signal box at the Wellington end of the station. *W.A. Camwell*

Stanier '8F' class 2-8-0 No. 48662 accelerates a westbound freight out of Gnosall on 18th July, 1964. In the foreground are the sidings comprising Gnosall's goods yard. No covered goods accommodation was ever provided here. Instead, unloading of wagons was performed on the concrete apron between the two sidings. *P. Ward*

Stanier '8F' class 2-8-0 No. 48347 pulls a down freight through the red sandstone cutting west of Gnosall in June 1963. This cutting was originally intended to be a tunnel of some 55 yards, but material was required for the embankment east of Gnosall, and so this was instead made into an open cutting. The bridge carries the A518 Stafford to Newport road over the line.   *E. Talbot*

An eastbound freight train approaching Coton, west of Gnosall, and about to pass beneath the A518 Stafford to Newport road. It is headed by an unidentifiable locomotive, possibly an LMS '4F' class 0-6-0. The open, rolling countryside is well portrayed here, with Windmill Bank rising in the background.   *LNWR Society*

roof, and a portion of the building next to the platform looks to have been cut out to let the trains pass beneath. This architectural curiosity was not repeated elsewhere on the line. The neat brick-built platforms were fenced by wooden posts with straight wire passing through. Economy seems to have been the watchword in the construction of this station, although as if to redeem this approach, the station platforms boasted some of the finest gardens in the country for many years. This may well have been the result of generous staffing, for there were three station staff at the time of closing, including the station master Stanley Griffiths, who was just 21 years old at the time. The station was actually situated at Gnosall Heath, but being only ¼ mile from the ancient town of Gnosall was quite convenient, and was just before the bridge over the A518 road. The cast-iron span of this bridge included the Shropshire coat of arms, and the SUR&CC company name. Unfortunately both the bridge and its abutments have been demolished. After the bridge, the line passed a small goods yard, which, whilst boasting two sidings and connections to both running lines, did not include a goods shed. A signal box was sited on the up side, opposite the goods yard.

Continuing on the embankment, the line passed round the back of a number of houses in Gnosall Heath before crossing the Shropshire Union Canal (actually the original Birmingham and Liverpool Junction Canal) on a substantial cast-iron bridge. Next, the line passed through two short, but quite deep cuttings before burrowing once again beneath the A518 road, and then out on to an embankment giving an uninterrupted view northwards for the next three miles. As the line passed the aptly named remote village of Outwoods, it was possible to get a clear view of Aqualate Park, home of Sir T.F. Boughey, Bart at the time of the SUR construction, and famous for its deer park. Also, at this time the engine crew would have their first glimpse of the Wrekin as it lies directly ahead, although still some 10 miles away. At this point the descent of the line had increased to 1 in 132, enabling the engine crews to relax for two miles.

In this area, an accident occurred on 22nd August, 1864 which is best described using the reporter's own words from the *Wellington Journal* of 27th August, 1864:

ACCIDENT TO A LUGGAGE TRAIN – On Monday last one of the luggage trains from Stafford to Shrewsbury, on the Shropshire Union line, got off the rails about two miles from Newport station. It appears that the train, which was composed of several luggage vans, had just entered on the decline which commences at Broadhill and reaches to Newport, and, from some unexplained cause, five of the vans, filled with various kinds of merchandise, got off the rails, cutting up the embankment for some distance, and eventually toppling over into the road beneath, a complete wreck. This accident caused the line to be blocked up for some distance, so that the passenger trains were a little delayed. By the assistance of several hands one of the rails was cleared, so that traffic was resumed on one of the rails to Gnosall. The waggons were smashed to atoms. This is not the first time, we understand, an accident has happened at this spot to a luggage train.

The train was evidently a goods train, and the cause of the derailment is likely to have been earth movement in the embankment causing at least a partial shift

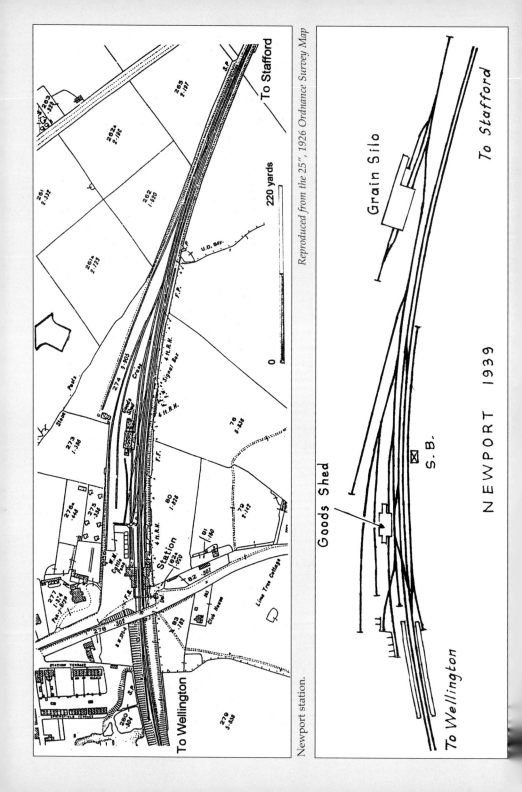

Newport station.

Reproduced from the 25″, 1926 Ordnance Survey Map

in the permanent way here, particularly as it is mentioned that several other accidents had occurred at this location, which was about a mile or so west of Gnosall.

Continuing, the line rolled over some flat agricultural land and arrived in Newport station (11½ miles). Now a market town with some local industry, Newport was not much more than a large village when the railway arrived, and is an example of the benefits derived from railways. First the line passed a large grain silo on the northern side, built by the Ministry of Food in the 1930s and subsequently considerably modernised. Rail access to the silo was gained from the goods loop line laid on the up side, which also served the extensive goods yard and goods depot. Cattle docks indicate the livestock traffic generated here, and an adjacent line served the works of the Newport Gas Light and Coke Co. Ltd, and local coal merchants. Nearby was the works of William Underhill, who started out as an ironmonger, but soon diversified into a foundry constructing agricultural machinery including stationary steam engines by 1870. In 1906, his business was taken over by the Audley Engineering Company, which had built its own premises nearby in 1869. This company later specialised in the manufacture of valves to control the flow of liquids, gases and powders. This later became part of the Serck group, and later still, became part of the BTR group. Incoming steel and outgoing valves, sometimes of huge proportions, added to the traffic through the goods yard. The refuge siding on the down side had capacity for 32 wagons.

Newport station displayed a further architectural style, this time being in blue engineered brick with stone quoins and built upon a more traditional railway style. However, the roofs were unusually clad in quite thick blue pantiles, giving a 'cobbled' appearance. The station buildings on each side of the line were of two storeys, and included the station master's accommodation on the down side. The main Birmingham to Chester road (now A41) crossed the line on an overbridge at the western end of the station. However, it is probable that originally this road crossed the line on the level, as the original signal box was situated on the western end of the up platform, in a position to control such movements. In 1877 it was replaced by a larger signal box, situated on the down side almost opposite the goods shed and adjacent to the down goods refuge siding. Also at some time before 1900 an additional canopy was added of a different design, giving a rather unco-ordinated appearance. A large, square brick-built stores building on the down platform was surmounted by a sizeable water tank, which served the water columns at each end of the platforms.

Leaving Newport, there was formerly also a lengthy siding on the up side known as Jones' Sand Siding, but this went out of use by 1925. The line curved south-westwards again, passing through a cutting for a short climb at 1 in 220, then out on to an embankment over some local watercourses, before running straight and descending first at 1 in 400, then 1 in 152, followed by a mile and a half of uphill running, mostly at 1 in 1,000 to Donnington. On the southern side can be seen the village of Lilleshall, and on the hill in its centre the 70 ft-high obelisk erected in 1859 to the memory of the 1st Duke of Sutherland (George Granville Leveson-Gower), who had founded the Lilleshall Company, and who died in 1833.

A roadside view of the northern side of Newport station around 1910, revealing the collection of buildings that eventually provided the station facilities, but clearly lacked a unified appearance.   *Shropshire Records & Research*

Newport station looking westwards around 1910. The heavy pantiles on the roof of the up side building are unusual.   *Shropshire Records & Research*

A view of the eastern end of Newport station *c.*1960. The goods yard is behind the wall on the left, with the goods shed in the distance, and the signal box a little further away on the opposite side of the line. The grain silo is partially obscured by the signal box.   *Lens of Sutton Collection*

Newport station viewed from under the road overbridge looking east.   *W.A. Camwell*

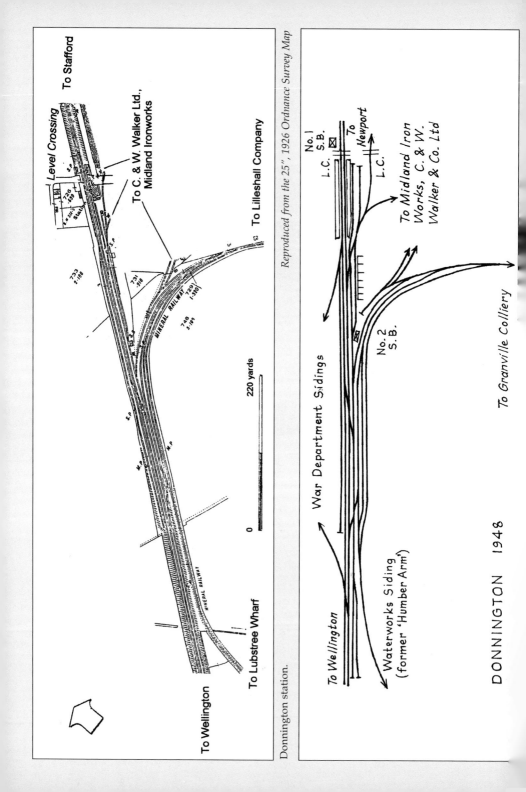

Donnington station. *Reproduced from the 25", 1926 Ordnance Survey Map*

To Stafford

Level Crossing

To C. & W. Walker Ltd,
Midland Ironworks

To Lilleshall Company

To Wellington

To Lubstree Wharf

MINERAL RAILWAY

MINERAL RAILWAY

0   220 yards

No. 1
S.B.

L.C.

To
Newport

L.C.

To Midland Iron
Works, C. & W.
Walker & Co. Ltd

No. 2
S.B.

War Department Sidings

To Wellington

Waterworks Siding
(former 'Humber Arm')

To Granville Colliery

DONNINGTON 1948

Donnington station (15 miles) was approached over a level crossing for a minor road, whose crossing gates in the 1950s were made of timber, but may have been replacements for the earlier SUR metal gates, which may have been damaged or worn out, as this road was much busier than the one at Derrington. Donnington No. 1 signal box controlled the crossing and was sited on the Newport side of the crossing, on the up side. The station building, on the down side, displayed a further architectural style, being of two storeys in red brick with white quoins and a slated roof. A glass canopy was provided for the protection of passengers, but only for the length of the station building, and so quite short for the entire platform. A separate brick 'gents' was also situated on this platform, along with a small wooden store. On the up platform was a brick-built single-storey waiting room with slated roof, and a store built of wood and corrugated iron. The station was named as Donnington from opening, but became Donnington Wood for a short period between 1st January, 1871 and July of the same year, thereafter reverting to its original nomenclature.

A small goods yard with coal drops was provided on the down side just to the west and south of the station, from which a line ran to the Midland Ironworks of C. & W. Walker Ltd. Next on the down side came the interchange sidings for the collieries operated by the Lilleshall Company, which under the National Coal Board comprised only Granville Colliery. Donnington No. 2 signal box was situated in the fork of the exchange sidings and was primarily concerned with control of traffic from these sidings to both running lines. There was also access from the Lilleshall Company's sidings into Walker's works. From around 1870, a further line ran westwards from the western end of these exchange sidings, then curved though 270 degrees to pass under the SUR line and proceeded to the Lubstree Wharf of the Shropshire Union Canal's Humber Arm, which provided transhipment for outgoing coal, and incoming lime for the Lilleshall Company's furnaces. This line was curtailed in 1924 just beyond where it passed under the SUR, and at this point became a headshunt for a new sand siding put in running southwards towards Wellington Road. This too eventually became redundant, and the remains of the line from the exchange sidings were removed during the 1930s.

Over on the northern side of the line, opposite to the Lilleshall exchange sidings, is the massive site of the War Department Central Ordnance Depot (COD), stretching alongside the line for about a mile. This was built over the site of the Lubstree wharf line and the stub of this branch was reinstated in 1938, until additional sidings were installed further west in 1940, with direct access into the COD from them. This group of seven sidings, along with the relevant access lines to the main running lines were controlled from Donnington No. 3 signal box, which was installed at the western end of the yard. The up refuge siding had capacity for 44 wagons.

This box was then less than ¼ mile from Trench Crossing station (16½ miles). This was a very simple affair, comprising a wooden gable-ended building with slated roof on each platform. The building on the down platform was slightly more substantial and included the booking office. At the Newport end of the platforms was a level crossing with the SUR metal gates (which in later years became rather dilapidated, as a result of mishaps with road vehicles),

An early picture postcard view looking eastwards along the platform at Donnington station.

John Alsop Collection

A view eastwards of Donnington station, revealing the neat station building with brief glass canopy, and the varying platform level on the down side, on which may be seen steps to assist passengers onto trains. Donnington No. 1 signal box is on the extreme left, which controlled the level crossing, whose original gates were unusually made of metal. The large building looming behind the station is the Midland Ironworks of C. & W. Walker Ltd.   *David Lawrence*

The up side platform buildings, level crossing and No. 1 signal box at Donnington around 1964. The passenger accommodation was surprisingly substantial in brick, whilst the small wooden building was for lamps and parcels. *P. Ward*

Stanier 'Black 5' 4-6-0 No. 45005 leaves Donnington and crosses the level crossing, which was protected by Donnington No. 1 signal box, with a train for Stafford in 1962/63. *A.J.B. Dodd*

The crossing keeper's cottage at Donnington, long disused for its original purpose. *W.A. Camwell*

Donnington's down side main station building was a pleasing construction, with heavy white quoins, and elegant chimneys. The adjacent small brick building provided almost open air facilities for 'gentlemen', and a small wooden store completes the ensemble.   *P. Ward*

The diminutive station accommodation at Trench Crossing, mostly located on the down side, and consisting of a wooden booking hall/waiting room and store. Between the two, the brick built 'gents' is clearly the most substantial construction. This view dates from the early years of the 20th century.

John Alsop Collection

Trench Crossing station looking westwards around 1964. The station remained lit by gas to the end.   *P. Ward*

A charming study at Trench Crossing station, as Fowler class '4' 2-6-4T No. 42389 waits with a Stafford train, and the porter attends to a lady passenger and her bicycle. The staff here evidently had time to keep their station platforms clean and the flower beds well looked after. *A.J.B. Dodd*

controlled from a small cabin on the down side. This station was the only one on this section of the line not in use at the time of opening on 1st June, 1849, not being opened to passengers until 1st January, 1855.

A quarter of a mile further on came the junction of the Wombridge branch, which was opened in 1866 to serve the Trench ironworks, the Shropshire ironworks, the Wombridge ironworks and several smaller industrial premises alongside the Trench branch of the Shrewsbury Canal (later part of the Shropshire Union Canal), and at the foot of the infamous Trench inclined plane. The continuation of this line from the Shropshire ironworks into Wombridge was abandoned after 1873, when a new and more convenient line was brought into use off the Coalport branch. However, the remaining works continued to be serviced by a locomotive from the small engine shed (see *Chapter Nine*) situated in the fork of the branch at Trench, opposite which stood Trench Sidings signal box.

Just over a quarter of a mile further, came Hadley Junction at which point the LNWR Coalport branch diverged southwards (see *Chapter Twelve*). Hadley Junction signal box was situated in the fork of this junction, and also had control over the sidings and movements to the Castle ironworks (see *under GKN Sankey Ltd, Chapter Ten*) which were located on the northern side of the line.

A further quarter mile on came Hadley station (17½ miles), located towards the end of over a mile of 1 in 166 uphill working from Trench. This was a fairly straightforward affair, of single-storey red brick building with slate roof on the up platform, and a small wooden waiting shelter on the down platform. The steps leading down from the up platform to the road level beneath were covered for part of the way. There were no goods facilities, and no signal box at the station. It is noteworthy that after the opening in 1861 of the Coalport branch, this station enjoyed a service second only to Wellington, as trains from both lines stopped here. A short distance further on, a footbridge was erected which was given the local name of 'the chocolate bridge'. Presumably, it was painted brown at some time, as any other reason for the name has not been found.

The line then curved south-westwards in a cutting, passing the Haybridge Iron Co. Ltd (established 1864) on the down side, for which a siding connection was provided from 1870. This was just before reaching the S&BR at Stafford Junction (18½ miles). There was an additional siding connection into the Haybridge Iron Co. Ltd from the S&BR line. Wellington No. 1 signal box controlled Stafford Junction.

The line is now that of the original SUR/S&BR construction onwards to Shrewsbury General. Just half a mile from Stafford Junction, the line runs into Wellington station (19½ miles), as it was originally known. It was renamed 'Wellington for Telford' on 16th May, 1983 and again on 12th May, 1986 as 'Wellington Telford West'. When originally opened, the down platform was just about as long as the main station buildings situated thereon. The present island platform had only a single face (for up trains) and was very much shorter, so that the western end of the up platform terminated more or less opposite where the eastern end of the down platform terminated. Thus, the use of staggered platforms facilitated the positioning of a boarded crossing for passengers and

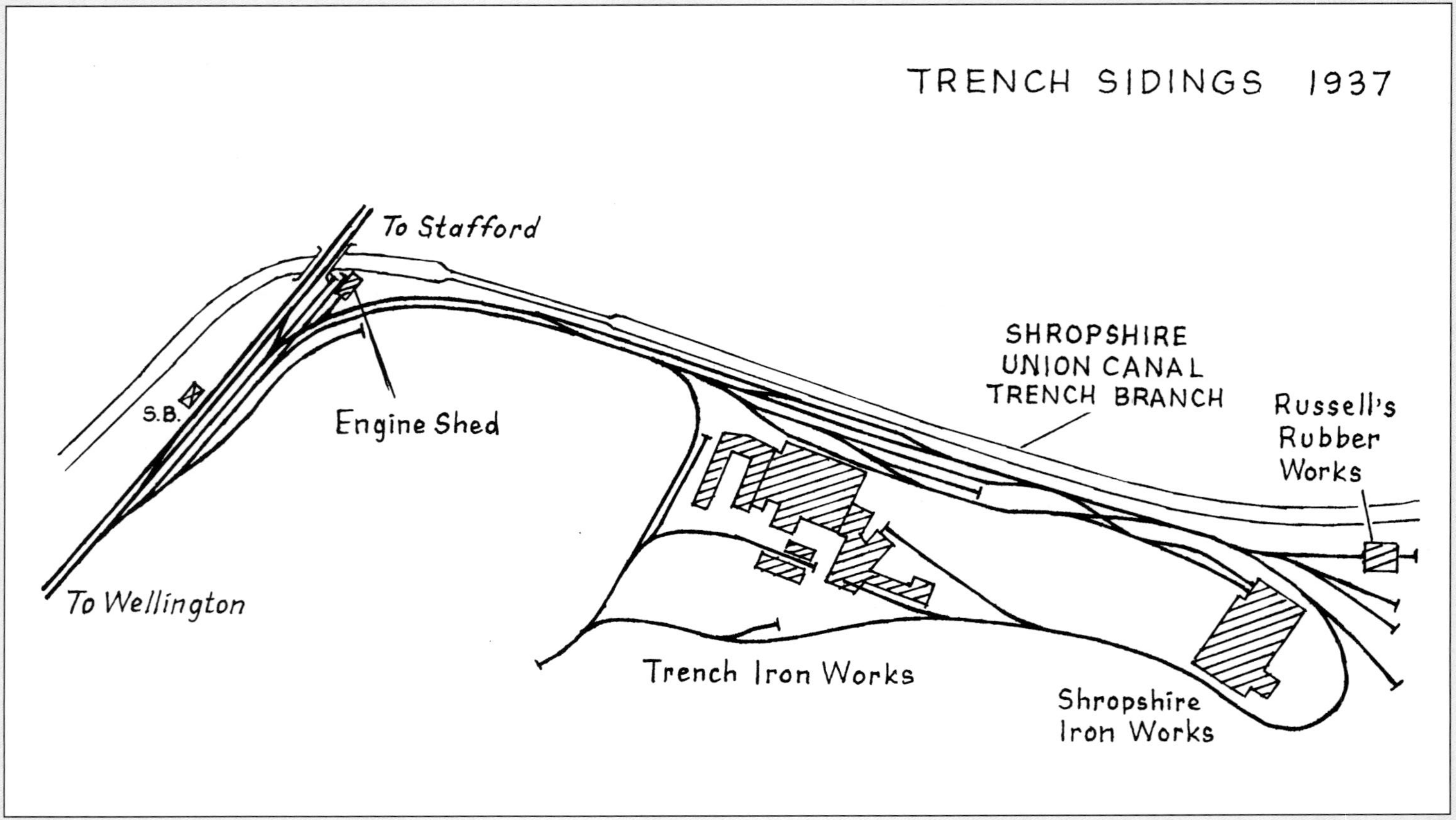

TRENCH SIDINGS 1937

Russell's Rubber Works

SHROPSHIRE UNION CANAL TRENCH BRANCH

Shropshire Iron Works

Trench Iron Works

To Stafford

Engine Shed

S.B.

To Wellington

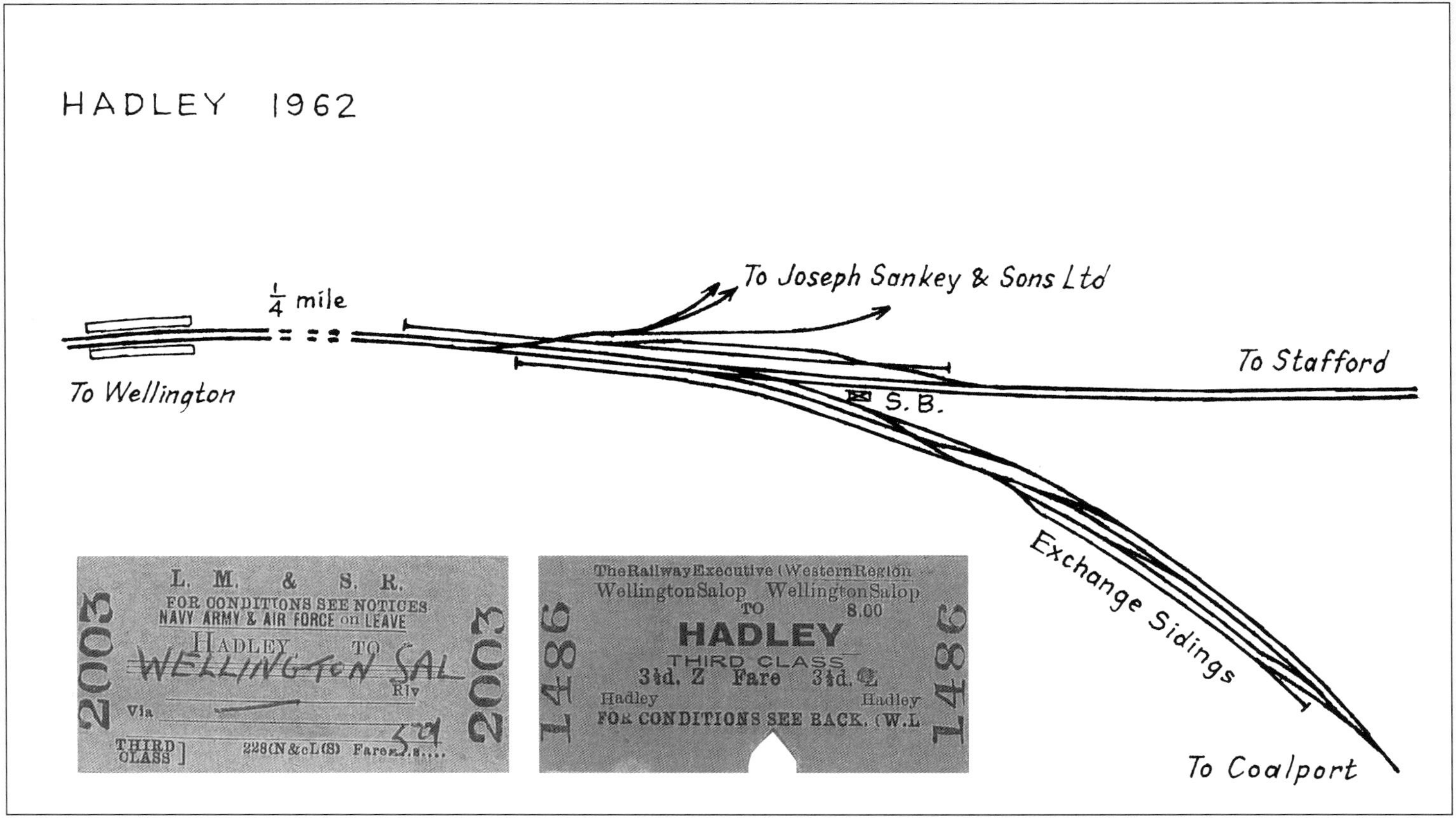

HADLEY 1962

To Stafford

To Joseph Sankey & Sons Ltd

To Coalport

Exchange Sidings

S.B.

¼ mile

To Wellington

The Railway Executive (Western Region)
Wellington Salop. Wellington Salop.
HADLEY
8.00
TO
THIRD CLASS
3¾d. Ø Fare 3¾d. Ø
Hadley   Hadley
FOR CONDITIONS SEE BACK. (W.L.
1486   1486

L. M. & S. R.
FOR CONDITIONS SEE NOTICES
NAVY ARMY & AIR FORCE ON LEAVE
HADLEY
WELLINGTON TO SAL
VIa   Rly
THIRD
CLASS]   2¾8(N &o L(B) Fare 5¾d......
2003   2003

Hadley station building on the up platform displayed considerable individuality, with its ornate chimneys and barge boards. This is contrasted by the very simple wooden waiting shelter on the down side. The top illustration dates from 1932 and the lower one is c.1960.

John Alsop Collection and Lens of Sutton Collection

The scene is Stafford Junction, Wellington around 1964, and in the foreground is Wellington No. 1 signal box. A Stanier 'Black 5' 4-6-0 is held at signals on the SUR line from Stafford, whilst on the right, a Stanier '8F' 2-8-0 approaches from the Wolverhampton direction. *A.J.B. Dodd*

Webb coal tank No. 7731 is about to pass under Victoria Street bridge with a local train on 3rd August, 1935. In the distance is Wellington No. 2 signal box. *H.F. Wheeller*

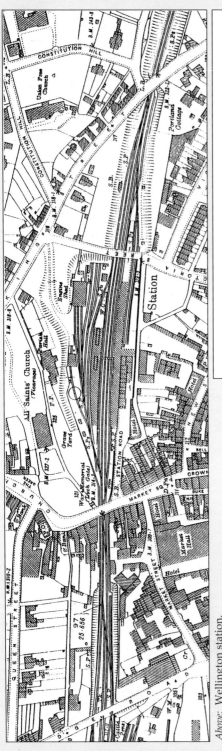

Above: Wellington station.

Reproduced from the 25", 1926 Ordnance Survey Map

Right: A request for tenders for major work at Wellington station that appeared in the *Wellington Journal* on 21st May, 1880.

LONDON AND NORTH-WESTERN AND GREAT WESTERN RAILWAYS.

TO BRIDGE AND ROOFING CONTRACTORS.

THE Joint Committee of the London and North-Western and Great Western Railway Companies are prepared to receive TENDERS for the CONSTRUCTION and ERECTION of a ROOF over the UP-PLATFORM and an OVERBRIDGE to CONNECT the UP and DOWN PLATFORMS, at WELLINGTON STATION, SHROPSHIRE.

The Drawings and Specifications may be inspected on and after TUESDAY, the 1st proximo, on application to the Engineer, Mr. R. E. JOHNSTON, Woodside Station, Birkenhead,

Tenders, endorsed "Tender for Work at Wellington," to be delivered to the undersigned, not later than 10·0 a.m., on SATURDAY, the 12th proximo.

The Directors do not bind themselves to accept the lowest or any Tender.

J. WAIT, Secretary.

Woodside Station, Birkenhead,
19th May, 1880.

staff, as no footbridge was at first provided. A goods shed and loading deck was initially available on the northern side of the up platform, but was subsequently rebuilt for use as an engine shed (*see Chapter Nine*). Goods facilities were subsequently provided separately by the GWR and the LNWR further west. It is believed that at some date prior to 1870, the two bay platforms on the down side were added. Around 1880, the main platforms were extended and a covered footbridge added. Wellington No. 2 signal box was sited just beyond the eastern end of the island platform, and Wellington No. 3 at the western end of the down platform. The station is overlooked by the parish church of All Saints, and although the present church is relatively modern, there has been a church on that site since the Middle Ages. It comes therefore as no surprise to learn that the building of the railway so close to the church actually meant that part of the consecrated graveyard was disturbed. In recognition of this, the patterns of the brackets supporting the down side (i.e. original) canopy incorporate crosses. Indeed, the outside of the adjacent Station Hotel, opened at the same time, was similarly decorated, although these have now been removed.

Wellington station is set in a cutting, and the line continues in this brick-lined cutting for a further quarter of a mile, until it bisects the site of the goods yards. The LNWR's large Queen Street goods depot was on the up side, adjacent to the livestock sidings of the Wellington Smithfield. On the down side, the GWR Wellington Town goods depot was served by a complex of sidings, which also served the substantial timber yard and premises of Richard Groom, Sons & Co. Ltd. This eight acre site was originally established by John Dickson in 1852 as his engineering works called Shropshire Works, producing a wide range of railway products including rolling stock and serving as the base for his railway contracting business. At this time he was building the S&BR Madeley branch, and later built the Wellington & Severn Junction Railway from Ketley to Lightmoor, which opened in 1859. A less well known project of his was the mixed gauge Wolverhampton Junction Railway of 1854, which ran for a mere ¾ mile from Cannock Road Junction to Stafford Road Junction, Wolverhampton. However, he is believed to have become bankrupt in the 1870s, and the site was taken over in 1882 by R.G. Groom (1818-1892) who had started a basket making business in New Street, Wellington around 1841. His son Richard developed the business on its new site to include sawmilling and turned wooden ware and bendware. As examples, their late 19th century product range included dollies, wooden bowls, butter boards, butter workers, butchers skewers, bakers peels, oval tubs, childrens hoops, toy spades, and heavy engineering timbers for use in the construction business. For this production, the raw materials were sycamore, willow, maple, ash and oak. Most of these materials arrived via the rail connection and the products were dispatched by the same means. Almost next door was the Wellington Gas Company's works, which again was rail connected, and was, of course, supplied with coal for making town gas.

Wellington No. 4 signal box was situated at the western end of these yards on the down side, and as well as controlling traffic movements for both yards, also controlled the nearby Drayton Junction, where the line for Market Drayton and Crewe diverged northwards. The line was built virtually on the level through Wellington, but now falls at 1 in 120 for nearly two miles until Allscott.

A general view of Wellington station from the eastern end *c*.1930. The train in the bay platform is probably awaiting departure for Much Wenlock.   *Mowat Collection*

A general view of Wellington station from the western end *c*.1932. The original coaling stage can be seen in the locomotive yard on the left, whilst the Station Hotel is on the right.
Mowat Collection

A view from the road bridge at the western end of Wellington station on 9th August, 1932. The GWR goods yard and cattle station are on the left while the ex-LNWR Queen Street goods shed is seen on the right.   *Mowat Collection*

Longsight-allocated ex-LMS 'Patriot' class 4-6-0 No. 45501 *St Dunstans* passes Queen Street goods shed, Wellington, with a Shrewsbury-Stafford train on 6th August, 1956. *Brian Morrison*

Reproduced from the 25", 1926 Ordnance Survey Map

Wellington goods yard area.

The massive bulk of the Wrekin looms up just about two miles to the south, and this is the closest that the line comes to it. Composed of volcanic ash, but not actually an extinct volcano as is often believed, the hill dates from the Cambrian period, more than 600 million years ago, and the summit is 1,335 feet. The line is heading north-west at this point, but soon curves in a cutting at Wrockwardine Bank to a westerly direction, and we reach Admaston station (21 miles), located towards the start of a two mile descent at 1 in 120. Not furnished with any goods facilities, this was a fairly basic station, although the station master's house, situated above the line and next to the main road, was fairly substantial. A sloping pathway for trollies and prams, and a separate set of wooden steps located alongside, gave access to the up platform. The signal box, booking office and waiting room were on the up side, and located, similarly to Haughton, beneath the road overbridge, in one of the arches. The down side comprised a single-storey waiting room, with access to the platform by a boarded crossing or via another set of steps from adjacent to the road overbridge. Admaston had Victorian aspirations to become a 'spa town', but it never really became fashionable. From 30th June, 1952 this station was downgraded and renamed Admaston Halt, reflecting its unmanned status. The signal box was closed on 28th February, 1954 when power operated intermediate block section signals were introduced, and operated from Allscott box.

Passing through rolling open countryside, the line comes to the site of Austin's manure works, where a single line was provided off the up line by means of a backshunt. A quarter of a mile further on, we reach the Allscott Works of the British Sugar Corporation, originally the Shropshire Beet Sugar Co. Ltd. Here there were goods loops provided for both directions, plus a fan of six reception/sorting sidings, from which headshunts led in to the internal railway system of the works, handled by their own locomotives. A signal box was sited on the down side opposite the mid-point of the reception sidings. Here the line is on the level once more.

One and a half miles further on was reached the village station of Walcot (23 miles). This station consisted of a brick-built two-storey station building with slated roof on the up side, and a simple single-storey waiting room on the down side. Because of the slope of the land here, the up side main building was of two storeys when viewed from the approach drive, but only one at platform level. No footbridge was provided here either, passengers having to make do with a boarded crossing between platforms. A signal box was sited some ¼ mile to the east, at the midpoint of the up side goods loop. The line now descends at 1 in 185 for over one mile, makes a slight curve to the right to correct its westbound direction, and passes over the River Teme on a red brick three-arch bridge of pleasing, but unexceptional appearance. Each arch has a span of approximately 25 feet. The line continues in virtually a dead straight line all the way to Shrewsbury, with a rising gradient of 1 in 150 for the first mile, then at 1 in 750 for another mile to the summit, thereafter dropping into the county town. But first, the line passes over the long abandoned Shrewsbury Canal, just as it enters Upton Magna station (25 miles), where the indicated change to an uphill gradient occurs. This station was rather more substantial than the previous two, and was provided with a small goods yard and goods shed on the up side.

Admaston Halt *c.*1960 looking towards Wellington. The station master's house is at the top of the bank on the left, and the former booking office is beneath the roadbridge out of sight behind the camera.   *Lens of Sutton Collection*

Admaston Halt view along the platform looking towards Wellington.

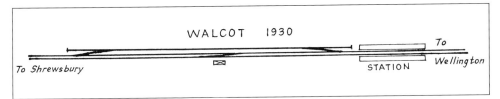

A view looking east along the platforms at Walcot.

A view looking west from the platform at Walcot. Unusually the station building was situated at the end of the platform. The signal box can be seen in the distance, it is sited opposite the goods loop. Access to the opposite platform was gained via the board crossing.

Lens of Sutton Collection

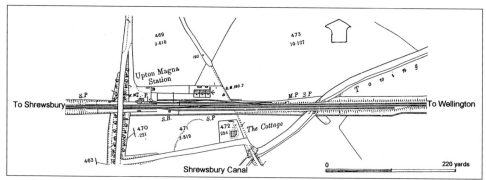

Upton Magna station.   *Reproduced from the 25", 1926 Ordnance Survey Map*

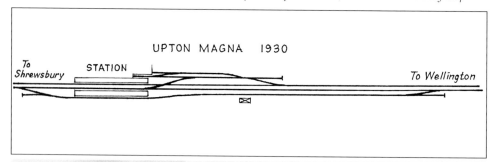

BR Standard class '5' 4-6-0 No. 73053 arrives at Upton Magna with the 5.24 pm from Stafford on 29th August, 1964. By this date the track in the former goods yard had been removed.

Millbrook House/D. Johnson Collection

The station at Upton Magna in 1962, viewed towards Wellington in the up direction. The principal station buildings are on the left, with the small goods yard behind. On the right, the down refuge loop can be seen running behind the platform, with its collection of roses adorning the fencing.   *Author's Collection*

A view along the platform from the western end of Upton Magna station looking east under the road overbridge *c.*1960.   *Lens of Sutton Collection*

Two views of the station building at Upton Magna on 30th June, 1962.   *(Both) R.M. Casserley*

There was a separate two-storey station master's house, and a two-storey station building was located on the up platform, with just a simple waiting shelter on the down platform. A boarded crossing was provided for persons crossing to and from the down platforms. The goods yard was controlled from a signal box on the down side opposite the yard, on which was also provided a down goods loop, which was passed behind the down platform. This loop was installed in 1909 to increase the line capacity, but was taken out of use in 1966. Additional goods traffic was anticipated from the nearby Beswick Wharf of the Shrewsbury Canal, although it is doubtful if it ever reached the expected levels. Instead, the rich agricultural land in this area would, over the years, have provided Upton Magna with a considerable traffic of inbound coal and agricultural machinery and outgoing arable crops and livestock.

The line recrosses the meandering Shrewsbury Canal bed just after the summit of the climb, near to The Manse, and then crosses the River Severn on the elegant Belvidere bridge, which was already described in Chapter Three. The line now enters a cutting and begins a half-mile climb of 1 in 150.

After passing under the Belvidere Road bridge, the line passes the site of Potteries Junction and the Potts Yards, and starts a descent at 1 in 130, passing under the Sparrow Lane bridge and Monksmoor Street bridge to emerge at the site of the original S&BR and SUR goods yards at Abbey Foregate. The S&BR yard was situated on the south or down side of the line, and contained a substantial goods shed, and a small single-road locomotive shed. Both of these were demolished long ago, but the yard continued in operation, concentrating mainly on coal traffic.

On the opposite side of the line, the SUR yard also contained a goods shed and single-road locomotive shed, both also long gone. On the rising ground to the rear of the yard once stood a small reservoir, for supplying water to the locomotive sheds, and although this apparently survived into the 20th century, this too has gone. This yard tended to concentrate on show and race ground traffic over the years, and both locomotives and carriages continued to be stabled in this yard past the turn of the 19th century.

The SUR goods yard was the scene of an unfortunate, but all too common, accident on 23rd February, 1933. At 5.40 am John Thomas Capestick, a carriage and wagon examiner, was stooping in the 'four-foot' between stationary wagons, looking at the draw gear on a wagon. He had been notified that shunting activity was taking place, but had placed himself in a very vulnerable position. Suddenly, a shunt of six wagons made contact with the wagon he was examining. The resultant impact threw him clear of the running rails and into the 'six-foot' between Nos. 4 and 5 roads. Unfortunately, his left leg was fractured in three places, and had to be amputated above the knee.

By 1864, the two goods depots were worked jointly under a Joint Traffic committee, although the LNWR had by this time built its larger goods facility at Howard Street Canal Basin, and in 1902 built its much larger yard at Coleford, just south of the General station, on the north-east side of the triangle and south of the river.

A joint station, originally titled Abbey Foregate, was provided here from the opening in 1849, although this appears only to have been used for the race specials and other excursions, as well as being a ticket collection point before trains entered

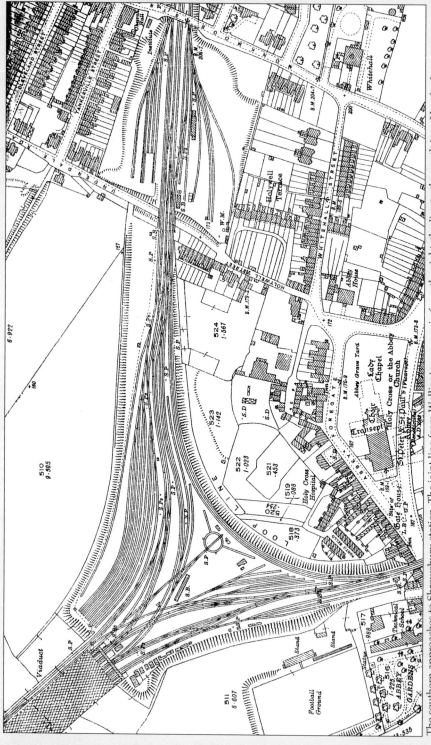

The southern approaches to Shrewsbury station. The joint line from Wellington comes in from the right, the line to the south is to Hereford.

Reproduced from the 25″, 1927 Ordnance Survey Map

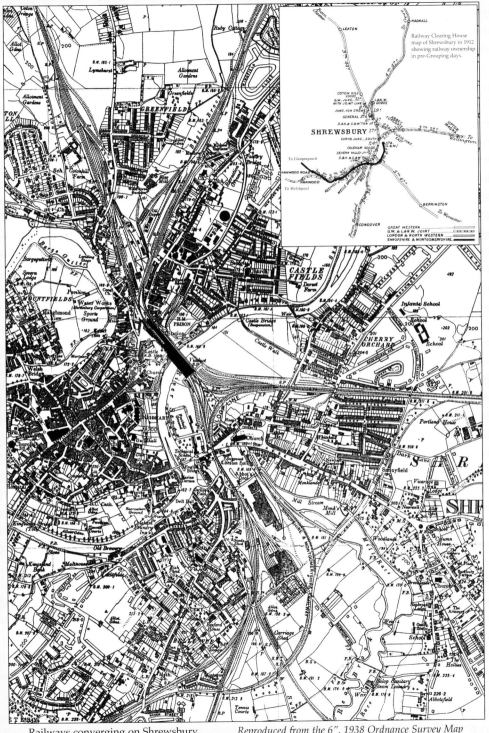

Railways converging on Shrewsbury.   *Reproduced from the 6", 1938 Ordnance Survey Map*

Railway Clearing House
map of Shrewsbury in 1912
showing railway ownership
in pre-Grouping days.

SHREWSBURY

GREAT WESTERN
G.W. & L.&N.W. JOINT
LONDON & NORTH WESTERN
SHROPSHIRE & MONTGOMERYSHIRE

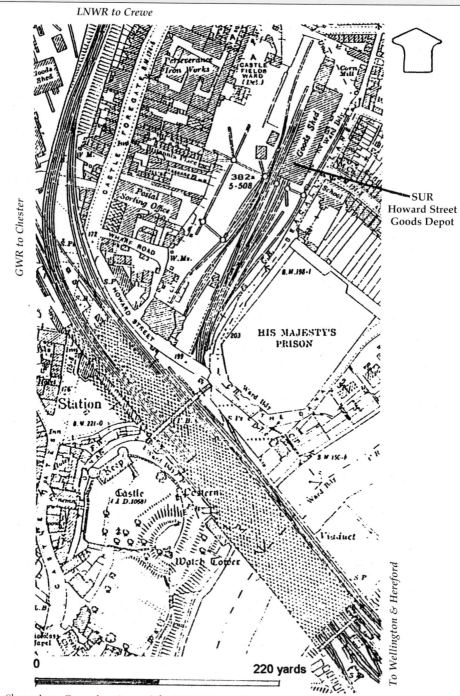

SUR
Howard Street
Goods Depot

GWR to Chester

HIS MAJESTY'S
PRISON

Station

Castle
(A.D.1068)

Watch Tower

To Wellington & Hereford

0

220 yards

Shrewsbury General station and the SUR's Howard Street goods depot.
Reproduced from the 25", 1925 Ordnance Survey Map

the General station. Certainly, by 1900 it was renamed Abbey Foregate Platform, and appears to have become little used so that it was closed from 30th September, 1912.

To control the traffic in the yards, as well as the spur to the southbound Hereford line, a large signal box was installed at Abbey Foregate, just by the site of the former Underdale Road level crossing. From here, the line is once again on the level. After joining the route from Hereford, the line finally crosses the River Severn and enters Shrewsbury General station (29½ miles). After Nationalisation, the station was renamed simply Shrewsbury. It had been built as a joint station by the SUR, S&BR, Shrewsbury & Hereford Railway and the Shrewsbury & Chester Railway to a design of Thomas K. Penson of Oswestry. The design was intended to complement that of the nearby 16th and 17th century Shrewsbury School (now the public library). Finished in Grinshill stone, the rather pleasing exterior has attracted several attempts at description of its architectural style, namely Tudor-Gothic, Tudor Revival and Neo-Jacobean. The construction was carried out by Thomas Brassey, who had won the contract with his tender of £30,963 11s. 2d. However, after taking into account the land costs and other extras, the final cost came out nearer to £100,000. The tower in the centre of the façade was furnished with an eight-day clock with a 12 ft pendulum by the notable makers, Joyce & Co. of Whitchurch, although this was not installed until 1850, after completion of the station.

To the south of the station, the Severn bridge was designed by William Baker, who it will be remembered was the Engineer for the SUR/S&BR joint line. Originally, it carried three tracks only, and consisted of seven elliptical arches each of 45 ft span, that were 18 ft above the springings and the rails were 36 ft above the mean water level. However, during the major reconstruction work on Shrewsbury station in the 1899 to 1903 period, the bridge was widened on each side by the addition of fabricated girders on cast-iron columns. These provided support, not only for the additional running lines, but also for the platforms that were extended over the river.

Returning to the station itself, this was originally constructed with two main platforms, each 16 ft wide. In the style of the day, there was an arrivals platform of 450 ft, and a departure platform of 650 ft. A 70 ft-span overall roof was supported on pillars at each side. The track layout and the early signalling were designed by Henry Robinson and Robert Stephenson. At the north end of the station, the four-track bridge over Castle Foregate was constructed of a 64 ft wrought-iron span by Brymbo ironworks. The subsequent opening, in 1858, of the Crewe line required an extra girder for the approach lines over Cross Street.

During 1861 to 1863 a new platform was added on the Howard Street side, and the original platforms were lengthened by 400 ft each. The arrivals platform then became an island platform. The existing roofs were extended by 250 ft, and a separate roof provided for the new platform.

Rail traffic continued to expand, and Shrewsbury became a well known bottleneck by the end of the 19th century, so that eventually a major restructuring was required, as already mentioned above. As well as the Severn bridge widening, the trackwork to the north was also revised, requiring additional girders for the widening of the Castle Foregate and Cross Street bridges, and major work on the station buildings. Most notable was the addition of an extra floor, not by building upwards, but by digging out the whole of the station forecourt, and then building

Work underway to add a third floor to the office and passenger accommodation at Shrewsbury station around 1900. The rather unique process of building underneath the existing building required the removal of the station forecourt down to the new level, so that passenger access to the platforms would henceforth be by subway.   *Shropshire Records & Research*

Fowler class '3' 2-6-2T No. 40058 arrives at Shrewsbury with a train from Wellington on 3rd August, 1953.

The view from the south end of Shrewsbury General station in 1959. The 180-lever signal box dates from the 1899-1903 alterations and was one of the largest in the country for many years, and still occupies its prime position. However, the footbridge has long since been removed.

Mowat Collection

Under the train shed at Shrewsbury General is Stanier 'Black Five' No. 45143 on 5th August, 1961.
Michael Mensing

Running alongside the train shed at Shrewsbury General is Newton Heath-allocated 'WD' 2-8-0 No. 90530 with a train of ICI ammonia tanks heading south. Note the ornate ironwork on the train shed roof.
Brian Morrison

A general view along the platforms under Shrewsbury General's train shed.   *David Lawrence*

Stanier 'Black Five' 4-6-0 No. 45298 at Shrewsbury General on 19th March, 1963. This engine was allocated to Shrewsbury and was used on the line to Stafford. Note the self-weighing tender which it was coupled to at this time.   *R.M. Casserley*

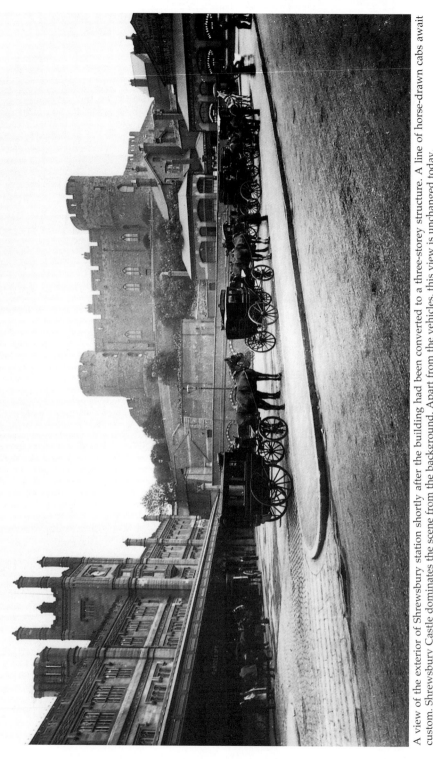

A view of the exterior of Shrewsbury station shortly after the building had been converted to a three-storey structure. A line of horse-drawn cabs await custom. Shrewsbury Castle dominates the scene from the background. Apart from the vehicles, this view is unchanged today.

this additional floor 12 feet *underneath* the existing building. So well done was this, that it is now only by close examination that this becomes apparent. The effect was that it was then possible to make subway connections to the various platforms directly from a new entrance hall, as well as provide badly needed extra space for the operating departments. The old departure platform was now 1,000 ft, with additional bays at the south end of 350 ft each (these were actually over the river). A new island platform replaced all the other platforms, and included bays of 450 ft at the southern end.

Subsequently, much of the old overall roof was removed in 1924, and partial canopies installed. These were in turn renovated and extended throughout the station in 1963.

Meanwhile, before the end of the 19th century, locomotive watering facilities and a turntable had been installed in the centre of the triangle south of the station, so that locomotive turning did not occupy the running lines, despite the existence of the triangle. A large signal box for operating the southern approaches to the station had been installed over the tracks on the Severn viaduct in 1880. However, as part of the major reconstruction at the end of the 19th century, this was replaced with the well known signal box situated in the middle of the triangle, which with 180 levers was one of the largest manually operated boxes in Britain.

One of the more unusual features of Shrewsbury station is the footpath, known as The Dana, which crosses the centre of the station from the Castle to the Gaol on a footbridge. This has no access to the station, but provides excellent views of the traffic below.

Shrewsbury station exterior in 1948 with a fine selection of British motor vehicles.

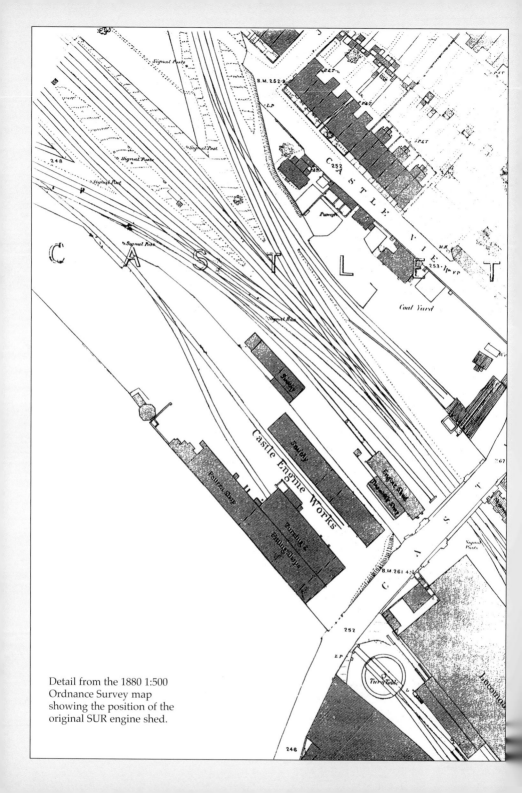

Detail from the 1880 1:500
Ordnance Survey map
showing the position of the
original SUR engine shed.

Chapter Nine

Locomotive Sheds

Stafford

A single-road locomotive shed was provided, although because SUR records are silent on this matter, the actual year of construction is not known. It is assumed to have been an SUR construction because of its position relative to the SUR line, being north of the station and the Castle Street bridge, on the down side of the line. On its eastern side, there was a further siding between the shed and the down running line. Later, the works of Messrs W.G. Bagnall & Co. Ltd were sited on its other, western side. The shed measured approximately 70 ft by 15 ft 6 in., with an inspection pit of around 25 ft placed north of the shed building, and another smaller building, labelled as a 'Tinsmiths Shop' adjoining its western wall. The track appeared to terminate just outside the rear (southern) end of the building. No turntable was provided, as far as is known. The shed was still in existence in 1880, as the 1:500 Ordnance Survey map from that year shows (*opposite*). However, it is uncertain as to whether it continued in its role as an engine shed at that time, particularly in view of the construction of the larger locomotive sheds, as we shall see. Nonetheless, by 1902 it had gone, and the site was given over to two carriage sidings, which continued in use into the 1960s.

This single-road shed evidently represented the sole locomotive facility at Stafford for a number of years, as Francis Trevithick (LNWR Northern Division locomotive superintendent) had petitioned the General Merchandise and Locomotive Committee several times for further locomotive accommodation at Stafford. He was finally given approval to build a shed to hold 12 locomotives in 1852. The building was erected shortly afterwards, comprising a four-road straight shed, sited just north of the station adjacent to the down running lines, but south of the Castle Street bridge. By 1854, 20 locomotives were allocated by the Northern Division to Stafford, and were presumably stabled thereafter at this new shed. However, after 1855, the SUR line's locomotives were provided by the Southern Division. It is unclear whether these were stabled at the original single-road shed or at the 1854 Northern Division shed.

An internal LNWR reorganisation in 1860 announced that Stafford was to be the limit of operations for both the Northern and Southern Divisions, and that an independent engine shed should be provided at Stafford for the Southern Division. The new shed was constructed in 1861 by John Parnell, for the sum of £2,750 10s. 0d., and was in brick with a hipped-roof of the typical design of John Ramsbottom, who by this time had assumed the role of locomotive superintendent for the Northern Division (and also the North Eastern Division). The new shed was of six roads, and was situated to the west of the 1854 shed. During 1862, the Northern, North Eastern and Southern Divisions were abolished; thereafter, common use was made of the two sheds. Subsequently, they became known as 'No. 1 shed' (1854 shed) and 'No. 2 shed' (1861 shed).

A general view of Stafford Shed in 1925. The No. 1 (1854) shed is on the right, and the No. 2 shed
(1862) on the left.   *John Alsop Collection*

Bowen-Cooke inside-cylinder 'Prince of Wales' class 4-6-0 LMS No. 5825 in the shed yard at
Stafford during the 1930s.   *LNWR Society*

Stafford became an important express passenger depot during its time as the border between the Northern and Southern Divisions. However, this distinction became somewhat blurred over the years with Crewe taking on the role of the major supplier of motive power, such that by the end of the 19th century, Stafford's role had diminished considerably. Certainly, by 1915 most of its allocation of main line locomotives had gone. As a result, in subsequent years, the sheds exuded an air of spaciousness.

The turntable, sited between the two sheds, was originally of 45 ft diameter, enlarged to 50 ft around 1866, and further enlarged to 60 ft in 1937/8. At this latter date, the crumbling 'No. 1 shed' was demolished, and a modern concrete coaling plant and ash handling apparatus (by Henry Lees and Co.) was installed. The 'No. 2 shed' was reroofed in 1947, and continued to perform its original function until 19th July, 1965 when it was finally closed. Thereafter, the building was initially used as a store, but mostly stood empty for more than 20 years, until it was entirely refurbished. It still stands, in use as the 'Palmbourne Industrial Park', housing a number of industrial units.

A view from Stafford station towards the coaling facilities at the engine shed on 23rd August, 1948. Ex-LMS Hughes 'Crab' class 2-6-0 carries its new British Railways number, 42944, but still bears the legend 'LMS' on its tender. Stanier 2-cylinder 2-6-4T No. 2616 is still carrying its LMS livery. The bridge in the distance carries Castle Street over the railway and on the right is the original Stafford No. 5 signal box. Just above the boiler of the 'Crab' you can see the hipped-roof of W.G. Bagnall's works. *H.C. Casserley*

Stafford Shed viewed from the west. Stanier 'Jubilee' class 4-6-0 No. 45571 *South Africa* stands in the foreground, with the coaling facilities on the right, and the ash handling plant beyond.
J.B. Bucknall

BR Standard class '5' 4-6-0 No. 73036 has left its Shrewsbury train at platform 6, for coal and water on Stafford shed.   *J.B. Bucknall*

Coalport

The brick-built two-road locomotive shed opened with the branch from Wellington in 1861. It was situated at the southern (terminus) end of the station adjacent to a two-road carriage shed. During the heyday of the branch in the 1890s, up to seven engines were stabled here, and for many years a turntable was provided alongside the shed. During 1924/25 one of the shed walls was substantially strengthened due to local subsidence. This necessitated large internal supports being constructed, such that the right-hand (westernmost) shed track was removed, thereafter giving the shed a somewhat cavernous interior and lop-sided exterior.

Throughout most of its life, it was a sub-shed to Shrewsbury, and was supplied with a diet of LNWR locomotives, mostly of Webb design, such as the '17 in. Goods' and 0-6-2 tanks, 'Cauliflowers' and 'Watford Tanks'. After Nationalisation, the shed was transferred to the Western Region, so that Wellington became the parent shed for staffing purposes. However, Shrewsbury LMS Shed (also transferred to the Western Region) was still responsible for a few years for supplying the motive power. So former LMS engines still dominated the branch, mostly in the form of Fowler 2-6-2 tanks for passenger duties, until withdrawal of passenger facilities on 31st May, 1952 at which date the shed closed. Both the engine and carriage shed remained empty and unused for several years, until being demolished sometime in the late 1960s. The site has since returned to nature.

Webb 17 in. 'Coal Engine' 0-6-0 No. 8148 outside the carriage shed at Coalport *c*.1932. The locomotive shed adjoined the carriage shed on its northern side.   *R.S. Carpenter*

Two views of the rather derelict looking Trench engine shed on 5th July, 1959.

(Both) R.S. Carpenter

Trench

This small single-road shed, constructed of timber with a corrugated iron roof is believed to have opened around 1870. It was situated on the southern side of the SUR running line, about ½ mile east of Hadley Junction. Trench housed a single locomotive, usually a short wheelbase 0-4-0 tank for shunting nearby industrial premises, including those situated on the Wombridge branch, which was opened by the SUR in 1866. These included the Trench Ironworks Company and the Shropshire Ironworks Company. Both of these companies were under the same ownership from 1872, making wire and wire rods, but the internal track mileages were considerably reduced during the 1930s in line with the shrinking of the factories. The private siding agreements for both sites were terminated during 1946. These industrial lines featured sharp curves hence the requirement for a small engine, which was supplied by Shrewsbury, the parent shed. For example, 0-4-0 saddle tanks of both Caledonian Railway origin and the former Lancashire & Yorkshire Railway (L&Y) were used. Certainly, LMS Nos. 16004 and 16027 (both ex-Caledonian) were used during the 1930s and 1940s, although LMS No. 11218 (ex-L&Y) was in use on 29th September, 1938. Earlier in LNWR days, Webb 0-4-0 tanks had been used.

The shed closed in 1943 as part of the wartime economies, as the volume of shunting was such that it was no longer necessary to out-station engines at Trench. The two sets of enginemen were transferred to Wellington, but remained under the control of Shrewsbury LMS Shed. Trench Shed was still standing in 1964, albeit dilapidated, but was subsequently demolished. After Nationalisation, Wellington provided the motive power for shunting as required, and as this no longer involved the tortuous curves of the ironworks, one of the standard GWR '57XX' class 0-6-0 pannier tanks was used. One of the remaining duties was to shunt the premises of Sommerfelds Ltd, steel fabricators. However, these larger BR locomotives were not permitted to cross the company weighbridge, which was situated just before a level crossing. The works line continued over this, then curved sharply and upwards into the works. Consequently, BR locomotives had to propel the wagons (often bogie bolsters) hard so that they would have sufficient momentum to clear the crossing and traverse some distance into the works sidings. The only means left to Sommerfeld of shunting from there into the works was by means of an ancient tractor!

The shed site is now occupied by the Trench Lock Interchange road complex.

Wellington

The locomotive shed was constructed by the SUR/S&BR for the opening of the line as a two-road goods shed, with one road passing through to the rear. It was built in brick with a slate roof, and was situated on the north side of the up platform at Wellington. Up to 1867, GWR locomotives had been stabled in fairly primitive conditions at Ketley. However, with the building of the line to Market Drayton, it was realised that there would be further locomotives to require servicing and stabling. This would be an ideal opportunity to improve the

Webb 17 in. 'Coal Engine' 0-6-0 No. 28204 outside the Wellington Shed on 21st June, 1947. This engine was withdrawn just three months later. *H.C. Casserley*

The three-road Wellington Shed on 26th June, 1964 showing a bevy of Collett '57XX' class 0-6-0PTs, *left to right*, Nos. 9630, 3744, 9724 and 3770. The wooden front gable end of the shed seems to have finally succumbed to over 100 years of attack from the exhausts of steam locomotives. *E. Talbot*

existing facilities in Wellington. So, in July 1867 the Joint Line Committee (by this time consisting of the LNWR and GWR) agreed to convert the goods shed into a three-road locomotive shed, as its use had been made redundant by the opening of the separate goods depots further west. The conversion work was completed by early in the following year, not too long after the opening of the Market Drayton line on 16th October, 1867.

For most of its life, Wellington Shed was the property of the GWR, supplying locomotives for local shunting and freight turns, plus passenger duties on the Severn Valley and Crewe lines. In the mid-1950s the shed received a small mechanical coaling hoist, protected by a structure of corrugated asbestos and sheet steel, as a replacement for its ancient coaling platform. At around the same time, the turntable was removed.

The site of the shed, close to the down island platform, meant that such activity as there was could be leisurely viewed from this platform. During 1961/62 several interesting locomotives were stored at Wellington Shed. One of the 10 Stanier 0-4-4 tanks, No. 41900, which had been tried unsuccessfully on the Much Wenlock branch was stored here until removal for scrapping. Around the same time, the last three GWR 4-4-0 'Dukedogs', Nos. 9004, 9014 and 9018, were stored here too.

The shed closed on 10th August, 1964 and was subsequently demolished. The site is at present occupied by track maintenance contractors.

The origin of Wellington shed as a goods shed can be seen in this view of the rear of the building. The locomotives on view are Stanier class '2P' 0-4-4T No. 41900 which was tried on the Wenlock branch and Ivatt 2-6-2T No. 41204. *J.B. Bucknall*

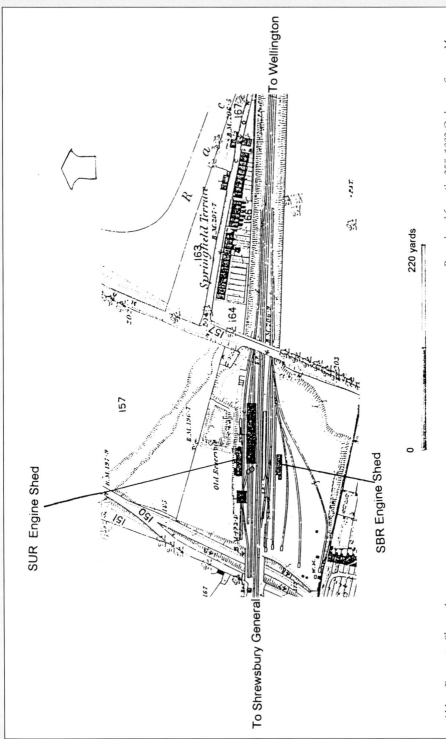

SUR Engine Shed

To Shrewsbury General

To Wellington

Springfield Terrace

SBR Engine Shed

0   220 yards

Reproduced from the 25″, 1882 Ordnance Survey Map

Abbey Foregate, Shrewsbury.

Shrewsbury

A single-road locomotive shed was provided by the S&BR on the south side of the line in its goods yard at Abbey Foregate. On the opposite (north) side of the line, the SUR also provided a single-road shed in its goods yard. Both are believed to have been opened with the line in 1849, but the SUR shed was no longer used for its original purposes in 1862, from when it became a wagon repair workshop. Both buildings had been demolished by 1918. A Shropshire Highways Depot now stands on the site of the former S&BR shed, and a low rise apartment block on the site of the SUR shed.

A joint LNWR/GWR locomotive shed was built in 1855 at Coleham for the joint Shrewsbury & Hereford Railway, which had opened in 1852. This was a five-road straight shed, brick-built with a slated, hipped roof. The LNWR occupied three roads, and the GWR the northernmost two. In their usual spirit of co-operation, a dividing wall was installed! It is not known at what date locomotives from the SUR began to be serviced and stabled at Coleham, but as conjecture it is suggested that passenger locomotives would have used this facility from its opening, whilst goods engines would have continued to use the shed at Abbey Foregate for some time, as this was adjacent to their goods yard.

However, by 1866 the LNWR had 51 locomotives allocated to Coleham, so that the accommodation was becoming too cramped (the usual, familiar story). Eventually, the LNWR erected a new 10-road straight shed in 1877 just to the south, as well as providing its own coaling stage and turntable. The new shed was built in the familiar Webb 'northlight' pattern, and was to retain its original roof until closure.

Meanwhile, the GWR soldiered on with the original five-road shed until 1883, when it constructed a roundhouse to the rear of this shed, roofed in the 'northlight' pattern and supported on iron lattice frames and columns. This shed abutted to the side of the 1877 LNWR straight shed. A new, standard GWR coaling stage was added in the yard also at this time. The two erstwhile GWR roads in the original shed were converted into a repair shop, and the erstwhile three LNWR roads continued as part of the GWR running shed, but also gave access to the roundhouse. Further locomotive accommodation was provided by the GWR in 1932, when its former wagon repair shop was demolished. A new three-road shed of steel framing and corrugated sheeting was erected on the northern side of the original 1855 shed.

To summarise the position at Nationalisation, BR inherited a very rambling arrangement that comprised three straight sheds totalling 19 roads (of which two were for locomotive repair shops), plus a roundhouse for which access could only be made through one of the straight sheds. No further modernisation was carried out at the shed, the depot being in a particularly decrepit state by the time of its closure on 6th November, 1967. The cleared site remained unused for many years, but has now been redeveloped for commercial purposes.

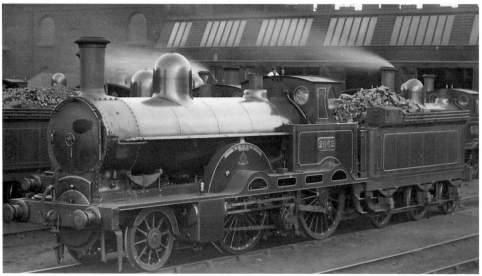

One of Francis Webb's notorious 2-2-2-0 compounds, No. 2062 *Herald,* of the 'Dreadnought' class is seen on shed at Shrewsbury in the early years of the 20th century.   *John Alsop Collection*

'Patriot' class 4-6-0 No. 45501 *St Dunstans* stands on the turntable at Shrewsbury Shed on 21st July, 1954. The northlight design of the engine shed in the background can be clearly seen.
Brian Morrison

Chapter Ten

Industrial Railways

The SUR served and was served by quite a number of industries considering its mainly agricultural route. These were mostly concentrated in the Donnington and Wellington area (now Telford). Whilst many rail served industrial sites were serviced directly by the main line companies, there were a number that possessed their own locomotives for shunting and/or movements within their own internal railway systems. These have been briefly mentioned earlier, and in this chapter are given more detail. Locomotives used at various sites are listed in *Appendix Five*.

W.G. Bagnall Ltd, Castle Engine Works, Stafford

This well known manufacturer of locomotives was sited just north of Stafford No. 5 signal box, the works extending alongside the LNWR Crewe main line and then alongside the SUR Wellington line. Rail access into the works was gained via a backshunt off the SUR line into several sidings, leading to different areas of the works.

The business was actually started by Bernard Massey in 1870 in premises in the centre of Stafford, possibly in Crabbery Street, and also in nearby Foregate Street. He carried on business as a brass and iron founder, agricultural machinery dealer and general millwright. He was joined about 1873 by John Hill, as a partner, and they carried on trading as Massey & Hill. Eventually the Castlefield site was leased from Lord Stafford and more suitable premises erected here, which were considerably expanded over the years. However, the partnership was dissolved on 30th March, 1875 and Hill carried on the business on his own. He must have been unwilling to carry the whole burden of the business and finances on his own, as in June of that year William Gordon Bagnall joined him, and the new partnership began trading as Hill & Bagnall. At this time Bagnall was only 21 years old, but had already amassed considerable business and engineering skills. After some early years working in a bank, Bagnall had undergone engineering training at Copper's Hill College, London and then spent some time working in his uncle's iron foundry of John Bagnall & Sons, Wednesbury.

However, the partnership did not last long, being dissolved after only a few months, on 26th February, 1876. The new business traded as W.G. Bagnall, although a new partner, one Thomas Walter, was introduced. Eventually, the business was incorporated as a limited company on 21st July, 1887. After his death, the business was initially acquired by Heenan & Froude Co. Ltd in July 1947 and subsequently by the Stafford diesel engine manufacturers W.H. Dorman & Co. Ltd on 21st January, 1959. In turn, they were taken over by English Electric Co. Ltd on 23rd July, 1961.

Bagnall had built his first locomotive in 1876, and went on to concentrate for the UK market on standard gauge four- and six-wheel shunting locomotives and

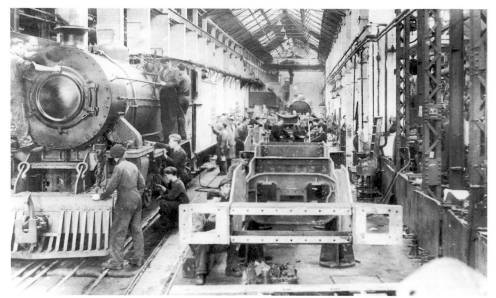

Inside Bagnall's erecting shop in 1951/2. On the left one of the order for seven metre gauge 4-6-0s for the Geakwars Baroda State Railway in India is nearing completion. On the right frames are being constructed for the order of 50 Hawksworth '94XX' class 0-6-0 pannier tanks for the Western Region of BR, which were numbered 8400 to 8449. These engines had a relatively short life, being ousted by the dieselisation programme, and many were scrapped after only around 10 years' active service. *Allan Baker Collection*

Looking south in the new erecting shop at Bagnall's works in 1956, production had switched to diesel locomotives. Those in this view were part of an order for 3 ft 6 in. gauge 0-6-0 diesel-mechanical shunting locomotives of 240 hp for the New Zealand Government Railways. *Allan Baker Collection*

narrow gauge locomotives of all types. For export business, particularly to the Commonwealth countries Bagnall tended to specialise in narrow gauge locomotives, and also provided the associated coaches and wagons. In some cases, the complete package for light railways included supplying the track as well. However, Bagnall only made limited forays into supplying British main line railways with locomotives. In 1926, 15 Fowler Standard LMS 0-6-0 side tanks were built (LMSR Nos. 16535 to 16549), and a further 10 in 1928 (LMSR Nos. 16675 to 16684). Between December 1928 and February 1929 seven more of the Standard LMS 0-6-0 side tanks were built, this time being supplied to the Somerset & Dorset Joint Railway (as Nos. 19 to 25, later becoming LMS Nos. 7150 to 7156). The GWR were supplied with 50 Collett '57XX' class 0-6-0 pannier tanks in 1930/31 (GWR Nos. 6700 to 6724 and 8725 to 8749). Between 1949 and 1954, British Railways Western Region was supplied with 50 of the Hawksworth '94XX'class 0-6-0 pannier tanks (BR Nos. 8400 to 8449), many of which saw less than 10 years' active service.

After World War II, Bagnall developed a range of diesel locomotives as well as its traditional steam locomotives. Production continued until the acquisition by English Electric in 1961, during which year the last locomotive was built at the Castle Works. The works is still intact, and is presently divided into industrial units.

No locomotives were ever specifically assigned by Bagnall to work within its premises, as it always had plenty of its own available on customer or stock order, to perform any required movements. New locomotives and those arriving for repair, and returning to their owners afterwards, were frequently seen being assembled into goods trains at Stafford including those running on the SUR.

C. & W. Walker Ltd, Midland Ironworks, Donnington

The works were situated on the down side of the SUR line at Donnington, just east of the station on the far side of the level crossing. Connections were made directly to the SUR line via the LNWR down side goods yard, and also to the Lilleshall Company's system at its exchange sidings.

The business was started as Charles Walker & Sons in Clerkenwell, London in 1837, where it manufactured stamps, presses and press tools. However, for reasons lost in the mists of time, it relocated to Donnington in 1857. The business was handed over to the two sons, Charles Clement Walker and William Thomas Walker, and was carried on as a general forge and engineering works, initially with a workforce of 35 persons. However, around 1868 they started making large gasholders and purifiers, and this was to become their staple business well into the 20th century. Charles was particularly well known locally, as he resided at the Old Hall, Lilleshall. However, he died in 1897, five years after his brother, and on 3rd May, 1899 the company was incorporated with limited liability, but retaining the brothers' names. By 1900, the business had grown considerably, employing around 800 persons.

During World War II, the firm manufactured steel plates for ships, heavy steel shields for large guns, bomb casings, mine destruction gear and other military hardware. In peacetime, production continued as before the war, but after the

Two views of Ruston Hornsby 0-6-0 diesel-hydraulic *Army 432* (Works No. 466623 of 1962) as it hauls a train of stores along the attractively landscaped internal system of COD, Donnington during 1990.   *(Both) P. Bushell*

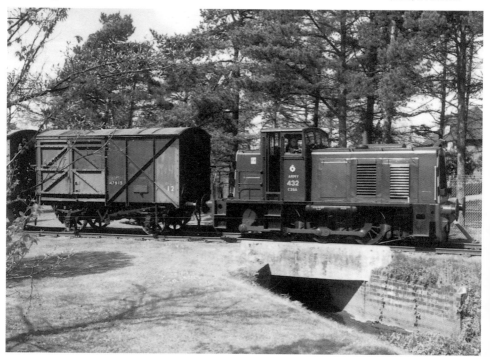

introduction of natural gas, the company used its knowledge of pressure vessels to move into the manufacture of petro-chemical containers for gases, liquids and solids.

For many years the factory buildings were clad mainly in corrugated iron, as the Duke of Sutherland (Proprietor of the land) had insisted in the terms of his lease that any permanent buildings must be capable of being easily converted into dwellings, in the event of the company's collapse. However, this requirement was never needed, and in fact the company purchased the freehold in 1942. A large clock tower stood outside the company offices for many years and, when the site was cleared in the 1980s, this was moved and re-erected in the centre of a nearby traffic island, where it remains today.

A curiosity of the company's internal rail system was a large circle of track in the area opposite the main factory, and behind Donnington station that was known as 'The Field'. Here the platework for the gasholders was brought out from the factory and assembled to test the construction of each such gasholder, before it was disassembled for transport to site and final assembly. This comprised the outgoing traffic, along with the purifiers. Rail traffic entering the works was generally sheet steel via the LNWR connections from the various suppliers, and coal and other steel and iron products from the Lilleshall Company. When the last locomotive left in 1952, internal movements were handled by one of the remaining steam cranes, aided by an ageing Fordson tractor, although rail traffic gradually dwindled in favour of road transport.

Ministry of Defence, Donnington Central Ordnance Depot

This massive depot is located opposite the site of Donnington station, although it continues for about a mile westwards. Construction of the depot was begun by the War Department in 1937, and the depot opened in 1938. However, it would be fair to say that construction continued for a number of years, if it has ever stopped!

By its very nature, little is known of the workings of the depot, as it was obviously subject to strict security. However, the internal railway system is known to have formed almost a complete circle within the depot, with lines disappearing into buildings with accustomed military precision. Although it was originally designated as a Central Ordnance Depot, it is now known as a Base Ordnance Depot. The depot experienced two major fires in more recent times, the first in 1983, and a much more serious fire in 1988. In both cases it was fortunate that the fires did not reach any stored ammunition (if there was any on site).

A locomotive shed was erected alongside the SUR line, adjacent to the main running line into the depot. After the A518 road was reconstructed on the trackbed of the SUR, it was possible to view the locomotives at close quarters. This locomotive shed, built of red brick with large glass windows along each side and a roof of composite material, is still extant, now being used as a maintenance depot for road vehicles within the depot.

The list of the locomotives known to have operated at COD, Donnington is sizeable, because of the policy of successive Army administrations in moving their rolling stock around the country on a seemingly random basis.

Ruston Hornsby 0-6-0 diesel-hydraulic *Army 432* passes one of the many level crossings on the internal system at COD, Donnington with a pair of bogie low loader wagons during 1990.

P. Bushell

Ruston Hornsby 0-6-0 diesel-hydraulic *Army 432* with a train of stores at Donnington during 1990. This was the sole working locomotive by the closure of the railway operation, as sister engines 420 and 427 were not serviceable.   *P. Bushell*

Lilleshall Co. Ltd, Oakengates

The Lilleshall Company's extensive railway system had exchange sidings with the LNWR at Donnington, just west of the station, and near to Oakengates station on the Coalport branch. The GWR also serviced the company's needs via exchange sidings adjacent to the GWR Hollinswood marshalling yard on the Wellington to Wolverhampton line.

The history of the company started with a partnership dated 8th September, 1764 between Earl Gower, John Gilbert and Thomas Gilbert to develop the minerals on the Earl's estate. This partnership was known as Earl Gower & Co. until 1786, when he became the Marquis of Stafford, and so the partnership became Marquis of Stafford & Co. until 1802. During this 38 year period, the coal and ironstone deposits were developed and canals were built as a means of transport both inside the estate, and with the outside world. One example was the Donnington Wood Canal which ran for 5½ miles from Donnington Wood to Pave Lane (near Newport), opening in 1768. By 1802, both of the Gilbert brothers had died, so the Marquis' son, George Granville Leveson-Gower, took over their share of the business. His father was now 79 years of age, so he relinquished half of his holding in the business to his son. The new business was established with a capital of £160,800, using the name 'The Lilleshall Company', after the family residence, Lilleshall Hall. In 1862 the company was incorporated with limited liability to become the Lilleshall Co. Ltd, and after quotation on the London Stock Exchange it became Lilleshall plc. It continued in this form until acquired by the Wyko Group in 2000.

The business continued to grow massively over the years, with the following coal and ironstone mines being opened: Hydraulic, Furnace, Rickyard, Lawn, Stafford, Dark Lane, Little Hayes, Lower Spring Village, Albion, Woodhouse, Hadley Nos. 1-7, Meadow, Waxhill Barracks, Lodge Bank, Barn Pits, Barnyard, Granville, Quarry, Foundry, Freehold, Muxton Bridge, Rookery, Grange, and Cockshutts. Not all of these were rail served and there were many other pits operated by chartermasters (i.e. the mining rights were leased to sub-contractors). By 1870 the pits were producing 86,000 tons of coal and 10,000 tons of ironstone per month. Iron furnaces were established at Lodge (Donnington Wood), Snedshill and Priors Lee, and steel was produced at Priors Lee from 1882 until 1925. By 1890, the Priors Lee furnaces were producing 700 tons of steel per week. Meanwhile, the Lodge furnaces had closed in 1888, although coke ovens at this site continued in operation until 1908, and coal screening until 1910. The Snedshill furnaces closed in 1830, although continuing as a wrought iron forge and rolling mill until 1924. Early brickworks at Wrockwardine Wood and Donnington Wood were replaced by more modern works at Donnington Wood in 1850, and the early Snedshill brickworks was continuously modernised throughout its life, lasting until 1977. The major engineering facility of New Yard engineering works was opened at St George's in 1861, producing mining machinery, including winding machines, boilers, and screening equipment, as well as blowing engines, locomotives, steam hammers, presses, water equipment and large gas engines.

In 1912, the German company Distillation AG erected coke ovens, and a by product and benzole plant at Priors Lee, although these were taken over by the

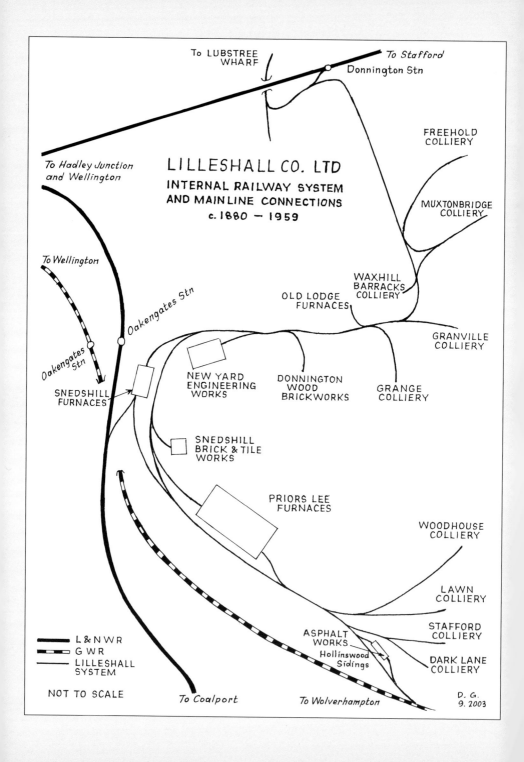

To LUBSTREE WHARF

To Stafford
Donnington Stn

FREEHOLD COLLIERY

MUXTONBRIDGE COLLIERY

To Hadley Junction and Wellington

LILLESHALL CO. LTD
INTERNAL RAILWAY SYSTEM
AND MAINLINE CONNECTIONS
c. 1880 – 1959

To Wellington

Oakengates Stn

Oakengates Stn

WAXHILL BARRACKS COLLIERY

OLD LODGE FURNACES

GRANVILLE COLLIERY

SNEDSHILL FURNACES

NEW YARD ENGINEERING WORKS

DONNINGTON WOOD BRICKWORKS

GRANGE COLLIERY

SNEDSHILL BRICK & TILE WORKS

PRIORS LEE FURNACES

WOODHOUSE COLLIERY

LAWN COLLIERY

STAFFORD COLLIERY

ASPHALT WORKS

Hollinswood Sidings

DARK LANE COLLIERY

—— L & N W R
▬▬ G W R
—— LILLESHALL SYSTEM

NOT TO SCALE

To Coalport

To Wolverhampton

D. G.
9. 2003

Government during World War I. The company acquired these works from the Government in 1920, although they were subsequently closed in 1938. As well as being used internally, coke was sold to the nearby furnaces of the Madeley Wood Company at Madeley Court and Blists Hill. Concrete works were established at Snedshill in 1903 on the site of the closed Snedshill ironworks, and adjacent to the wire rod mill. This new works produced precast blocks, slabs, and fence posts, and from 1917 pit props. This works was considerably expanded during the 1920s and 1930s. Meanwhile, the company had obtained leases on land for quarrying limestone at Presthope, near Much Wenlock, and at Nantmawr, near Llanymynech, necessary for its iron and steel furnaces.

Another German firm, A. & E. Albert, opened an asphalt plant near Priors Lee in 1912, using slag from the nearby furnaces, which was crushed and screened, then coated with tar from the Distillation Plant to form a roadmaking material. Later, fertiliser was also produced from the slag, which found a ready market in the nearby Shropshire agricultural industry. This plant was also acquired from the Government in 1920, having been similarly sequestered during the World War I. It closed along with the Priors Lee furnaces in 1959. During World War I, the engineering works produced shells, and the same were produced during World War II, as well as tank track links and bullet proof rivets for tanks.

The remaining coal mine was nationalised on 1st January, 1947 and so Granville Colliery became part of the National Coal Board. The blast furnaces and rolling mills were initially nationalised by the Act of 1949. However, this hasty piece of legislation was repealed under the 1953 Act, and they were re-acquired by the company. By the 1950s the New Yard Engineering Works was producing bottle packing machinery and modular steel buildings aside from its traditional heavy engineering works, which were declining considerably.

The reader will by now have gained some idea of the wide variety of the company's business. The accompanying map will give some idea of the way in which these activities were spread across the surrounding countryside. Most of the activities were linked through their production and involved the movements of large tonnages of materials, and so the reason for an industrial railway becomes apparent. The internal railway system was started around 1851 and eventually grew to cover 26 miles of track, and utilised 200 main line and 250 internal user wagons. Over the years, 22 locomotives were used on the system, of which six were built by the company, although none after 1900. The company built at least a further 34 locomotives for its customers. Locomotive sheds were provided at the New Yard Engineering Works and at the Priors Lee furnaces, but not at any of the mines. Wagon repairs were also undertaken at the New Yard Works using timber from the company sawmill.

In January 1858 an unusual accident occurred at Priors Lee relating to a locomotive hauling coal wagons to the furnaces there. The driver, Robert Munslow, had stopped at a level crossing, and as the keepers were away at lunch, decided to open the gates himself. Having dismounted from his engine, he operated the gates, but somehow managed to get in front of his moving engine and was run over by it and killed. He had evidently left it in gear, and without ensuring that the brake was properly applied.

Lilleshall Company, Oakengates. One of the company's own-built locomotives, 0-4-0ST No. 4 *Constance* (built 1865), stands outside the running shed at Priorslee Furnaces on 19th June, 1954. The company also made use of several former GWR locomotives, and behind can be seen their No. 5. This started life as a Barry Railway No. 60, a 'B1' class 0-6-2T, being built by the Vulcan Foundry in 1892 (Works No. 1342). It subsequently became GWR No. 251, until acquired by the Lilleshall Company in July 1934.

F.W. Shuttleworth

One other former GWR locomotive acquired by the Lilleshall Company was Dean '2721' class 0-6-0PT No. 2794. This was originally built as a saddle tank, and converted to a pannier tank in March 1916. After acquisition from BR in October 1950 it retained its cabside GWR numberplates, but also bore the painted legend 'Lilleshall Co. Ltd. No. 12' on its tank sides. It is seen here at the Priorslee Furnaces on 19th June, 1954.

F.W. Shuttleworth

The quality of mined coal was generally very good, such that the principal customers of the collieries were the LNWR (later the LMSR), the Cambrian Railways, and the GWR, for locomotive use. With the opening of the nearby power station at Ironbridge in 1932, coal was also supplied there.

The first part of the railway system to close was the branch from Donnington exchange sidings that continued westwards, then swung through 270 degrees to travel northwards, beneath the SUR and on to the Lubstree Wharf of the SUR&CC Humber Arm Canal. This transhipment point had been used since around 1870 for incoming limestone from Llangollen and from the company's quarries at Nantmawr (some also came by rail), and outgoing shipments of coal and pig iron. However, this fell into disuse after World War I, and was closed in 1924. A short portion on the southern side of the SUR was retained for access to a sand siding, but this was soon taken up. Afterwards, the land was sold principally for agricultural use, but much was later used for building the Central Ordnance Depot. The bridge under the SUR had remained in place, and was once more pressed into use as a rail access to the depot. It still exists, as a bridge under the A518 road, and is the main vehicular entrance to the depot. In March 1959 the Priors Lee furnaces was closed, as only one furnace was still usable. That required a major refurbishment, and even so was considered obsolete. Without the Priors Lee furnaces requiring coal, there was no traffic from Granville Colliery to this, the southern part of the system, nor would there be any traffic of iron ore and pig iron through the main line exchanges. As a result, the internal railway system closed. A final railtour was organised, running from St George's to Snedshill brickworks and on to Priors Lee furnaces. The three remaining locomotives were scrapped on site.

National Coal Board, Granville Colliery

Output from this mine after Nationalisation was always routed to the exchange sidings at Donnington, some 1½ miles away. This involved an awkward journey, as not only were there considerable gradients on the descent to Donnington, but all trains had to reverse at Muxton Bridge Colliery until a new direct line was constructed in the 1960s eliminating the need for reversal. At the colliery sidings the locomotives had to run round their wagons before propelling them over the weighbridge and into the washery for loading. Nearby, the Lilleshall Company's line from Oakengates made an end-on junction, adjacent to the Lodge spoil tip, where exchange sidings were provided. This company still retained running powers over the NCB line to Donnington, at least until 1955, but it was rarely ever used. Furthermore, as no engine shed had ever been provided by the Lilleshall Company, the NCB initially erected a flimsy structure of corrugated iron, but this only lasted a few years before it unsurprisingly blew down. So a new building of red brick, glass and a composite roof was built in the 1950s near to the colliery sidings, sufficient to hold four locomotives.

Much of the output was latterly destined for power stations, including the nearby Ironbridge 'B' station, so was marshalled at Donnington for collection in lengthy trains by the BR locomotives. However, the colliery closed in May, 1979 and the final train ran on 2nd October, 1979.

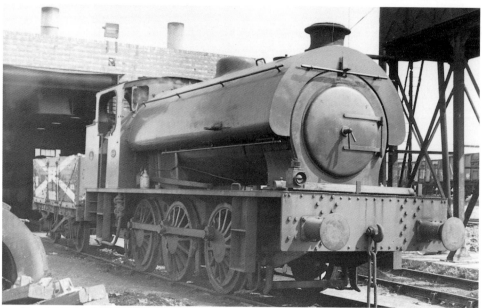

Hunslet 18 in. 0-6-0ST No. 3 (Works No. 3789 of 1953) stands outside the shed at Granville Colliery on a very hot 21st August, 1967 between duties. It had only arrived at Granville some two months earlier, from nearby Cannock Wood Colliery and was in superb condition.

Allan C. Baker

This Hunslet 18 in. 0-6-0ST (Works No. 2895 of 1943) was originally supplied to the War Department, and arrived at Granville around the middle of 1947 still bearing its WD number, 75046. Here it is seen on 20th March, 1969 after fitment of a Giesl oblong ejector, shunting an internal user wagon at Granville Colliery sidings.

Allan C. Baker

Hunslet 18 in. 0-6-0ST *Granville* No. 5 stands in the Lodge sidings at Granville Colliery as a similar locomotive shunts spoil wagons, around 1960.   *A.J.B. Dodd*

The steam locomotives at Granville were replaced by 325 hp Hunslet 0-6-0 diesel mechanical locomotives. Shown here is Hunslet's No. 6664 of 1969, carrying the running number 2D, and standing at the side of the weighbridge in Granville Colliery yard on a wintry day, 6th January 1970.   *Allan C. Baker*

LNWR 17 in. 'Coal Engine' No. 45 (later LMS No. 8149) posed with a train of open top tramcars from G. F. Milnes & Co. Ltd, Hadley Castle Car Works for Blackburn Corporation and mounted on special low bogie wagons. The location is believed to be in the sidings opposite the Hadley Castle Works, and the date is around 1900.   *LNWR Society*

North British 0-4-0 Mark I diesel-hydraulic (No. 27414 of 1954) seen at the Telford Steam Railway, Horsehay on 28th May, 2001, awaiting installation of a new engine. This locomotive provided motive power for the internal railway system of GKN Sankey Ltd at their Hadley Castle Works from July 1957 until March 1976 when it passed into preservation.   *Author*

GKN Sankey Ltd, Hadley Castle Works, Hadley

The Castle Iron Works was originally established on this site by the Birmingham company of Nettlefold & Chamberlain in 1871 to make bar iron and wire. However, the company moved its main manufacturing base to South Wales in 1886. The works were taken over on a mortgage as a going concern by Benjamin Talbot and his son of the same name. However, the business foundered and by November, 1888 they were declared bankrupt. The works remained empty and became increasingly derelict until January 1899 when they were purchased by G.F. Milnes & Co. Ltd, of Birkenhead. The old works were demolished, and a brand new factory erected by Hughes & Stirling of Liverpool for the manufacture of tram cars was opened in June 1900. Production started immediately, and by 1901 the 'Castle Car Works' (as it was now renamed) employed around 750 persons. Changes in the market for tram cars brought about the voluntary closure of the works in May 1904 by which time around 1,600 tramcars had been built there.

A reorganisation of the railway rolling stock industry in the ensuing years brought about the reopening of the works in July 1905 by the Metropolitan Amalgamated Railway Carriage & Wagon Co. Ltd of Birmingham. During the next three years, 133 carriages and 1,036 wagons were constructed at Hadley, until once again lack of orders forced its closure in 1908.

The works remained empty, but cared for, during the next two years until Joseph Sankey & Sons Co. Ltd purchased the property on 1st January, 1911. The site was used for the manufacture of motor vehicle wheels and body parts, becoming part of Guest, Keen & Nettlefolds Ltd in 1920. The company continued to expand (and still does!) over the years, as additional products such as beer barrels, racking equipment, steel office furniture, vending machines, vehicle chassis and military and agricultural vehicles were turned out. Amongst other wartime hardware, during World War II there were 868 Spitfires erected here. By the 1970s the site covered over 50 acres and employed some 7,000 persons. The company became GKN Sankey Ltd in 1968, and continues to operate successfully from this site.

Locomotives were used for the movement of incoming supplies, principally coal and steel, from the exchange sidings adjacent to the up line of the SUR, almost opposite Hadley Junction at the divergence of the Coalport branch. During the 1950s this comprised steel from South Bank Works, Middlesbrough and rim bar from Port Talbot. Coal was sourced locally, mainly from Madeley Wood Colliery, with Granville Colliery surprisingly only rarely providing supplies. Outward rail shipments of wheels went to the British Motor Corporation at Bathgate, and to Vauxhall at Liverpool. Export shipments were made in closed vans to the docks at Birkenhead and Liverpool. During the early 1970s, the development here of the Saracen armoured fighting vehicle led to anticipation that the majority of production would be moved by rail. Therefore, the rail link was retained, even though it was actually little used. In the event, it was no longer required, and rail traffic ceased here entirely during 1972.

None of the earlier inhabitants of the site had possessed their own locomotives, all shunting being performed by the LNWR locomotives. Indeed, it was only the wartime activities at this site that spurred the use of locomotives, initially by the Ministry of Supply, and later by GKN Sankey.

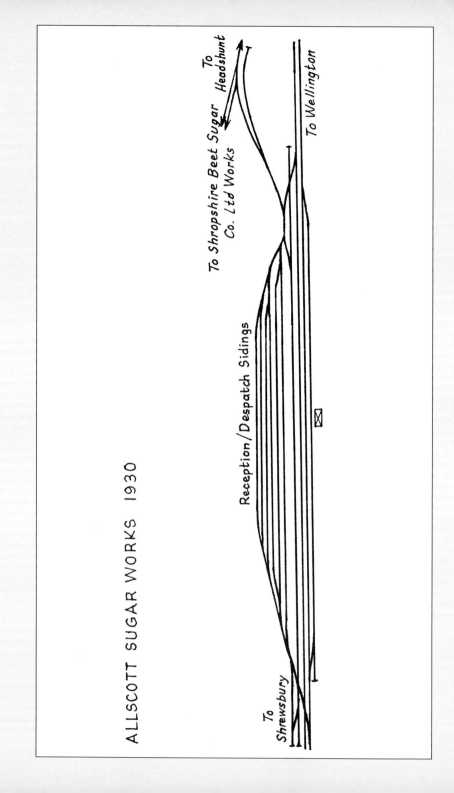

ALLSCOTT SUGAR WORKS 1930

To Shropshire Beet Sugar
Co. Ltd Works

To Headshunt

To Wellington

Reception/Despatch Sidings

To Shrewsbury

British Sugar Corporation Ltd - Allscott Beet Sugar Factory

The factory was opened by the Shropshire Beet Sugar Co. Ltd in 1927, ownership passing to the British Sugar Corporation on 12th June, 1936. A layout of six reception/sorting sidings was provided on the northern side of the joint SUR S&BR line, from which headshunts gave access to the internal sidings of the sugar works. The main incoming traffic was obviously sugar beet, which was loaded at various country sidings and was tripped as necessary to the works. This being a seasonal crop, most of the incoming traffic was carried in the months of October to January. Other incoming traffic consisted of coal for the boilers, limestone used in the refining process and coke for melting the limestone, also stores of just about every description as virtually all of the factory requirements came by rail. Outgoing traffic consisted of bagged refined sugar and animal feed in vans, and molasses which was shipped in heated tanker wagons.

During the harvest season (known as the 'campaign'), traffic of beet sugar into the sidings and thence into the factory was very intense. Two company locomotives were required, working round the clock, moving wagons to and from the exchange sidings. Furthermore the boilers had to be kept supplied with coal from that which had been stockpiled during the quiet part of the year. Final positioning of individual wagons within the works was performed by the use of powered capstans.

The use of road transport eventually rendered the rail system redundant, and rail traffic ceased in July 1983. The BR exchange sidings were taken up by November 1984 and most of the land was subsequently acquired by British Sugar.

Bagnall 0-6-0ST *Lewisham* (Works No. 2221 of 1927) was built locally in Stafford and worked at the British Sugar Corporation, Allscott Beet Sugar Factory from new until its retirement for preservation in 1970. Here it is seen in a rather woebegone condition, but still officially as 'spare engine', alongside the locomotive shed, and next to one of the steam cranes, on 26th June, 1966.   *Allan C. Baker*

The earlier Hudswell, Clarke 0-6-0T *Yorkshire* (Works No. 1070 of 1914) at Allscott Beet Sugar Factory was replaced in 1951 by this Ruston Hornsby Model 165DS 0-4-0 diesel-mechanical locomotive (304474 of 1951), seen here shunting in the snow of early 1970. From its arrival, it became the principal source of motive power, with the Bagnall *Lewisham* only being required during overhaul of the diesel, and during the intense activity of the beet sugar 'campaign' period each year.   *Allan C. Baker*

Bagnall 0-6-0ST *Lewisham* was constructed at the Castle Engine Works in Stafford (Works No. 2221) in June 1927 for use at the Shropshire Beet Sugar Co. Ltd (later British Sugar Corporation) at their Allscott works. It remained in use until October 1970 when it was presented to the Foxfield Railway at Dilhorne, near Stoke-on-Trent, for preservation. It was subsequently restored to full working order, and is seen here at that railway's Blythe Bridge terminus in sparkling condition on 25th July, 1993.   *Author*

Chapter Eleven

Closure and the Line Today

After Nationalisation, the Stafford to Wellington section had remained in the hands of the then new London Midland Region, whilst the Wellington to Shrewsbury line not unnaturally came under the auspices of the Western Region administration. However, as from 1st June, 1963 Shrewsbury and the entire line to Wolverhampton became part of the London Midland Region. From 12th February, 1966 control was vested in the Stoke district of the LMR.

The line continued to provide a valuable diversionary route, especially during the years of electrification on the West Coast Main Line, and particularly whilst the Stafford to Crewe section was being modernised. However, after completion of this work, it was clear that with dwindling passenger receipts, the future of the line was increasingly uncertain.

Closure of the line was a gradual affair, starting in 1964 and being finally completed in 1991. Apart from Haughton station, which closed to passengers as from 23rd May, 1949, all other stations on the Stafford to Wellington section remained open until closure to passenger services throughout on 7th September, 1964. The final train actually ran on the previous day, Sunday 6th September, 1964, as the 10.55 pm Wellington to Stafford and was formed of a Derby 'lightweight' two-car diesel multiple unit. Although the train was far from full, the *Newport and Market Drayton Advertiser* reported that a crowd of around 40 people, including the station master, Frank Clough, assembled on Newport station to bid farewell to their passenger service.

Local efforts to save the passenger service only appear to have gathered momentum during the last couple of months prior to closure. Furthermore, there seems to have been little support, and the movement faded quite quickly. Subsequently, and perhaps predictably, the passing of the local goods services produced even less reaction. Within weeks of closure, the local councils for Gnosall and Newport were looking at plans to convert the trackbeds into roads.

Freight services at Haughton had been withdrawn on 5th August, 1957 but Gnosall was not closed to freight until 1st June, 1964 actually before its passenger services were terminated. Donnington was the next to lose its freight services, on 4th October, 1965 but the line remained open throughout until the Stafford to Donnington section was closed completely on 1st August, 1966 (although not officially until July 1967). However, the track was not removed until the early months of 1970.

Towards Wellington, both Trench Crossing and Hadley had never offered any freight services, so although the line remained open from Wellington to Donnington there was no public freight traffic. Instead, the remaining traffic served the private sidings of GKN Sankey Ltd at Hadley, Sommerfelds Ltd at Trench, and the Ordnance Depot and Granville Colliery at Donnington. The stub of the Wombridge branch serving Sommerfelds at Trench was finally closed on 27th April, 1968. The sidings serving GKN Sankey remained in place until February 1984 although rail traffic into the works ceased during 1972.

In 1966, passenger working had already ceased two years earlier, but coal workings from Granville Colliery continued. Here at Donnington down exchange sidings, Wellington shed's Collett '57XX' class 0-6-0PT No. 9630 shunts the wagons of a recently arrived string of empties, whilst a Stanier '8F' 2-8-0 waits to leave with loaded train.   *P. Ward*

During 1971 the line from Stafford Junction, Wellington, to the Ordnance Depot and NCB exchange sidings at Donnington had been singled, this coming into effect on 25th July, 1971. Rather surprisingly, the first quarter mile of the Coalport branch, which incorporated sorting sidings, also remained in place after the singling of the line, forming additional siding capacity. Traffic continued to the NCB sidings at Donnington until 2nd October, 1979. Thereafter, the remaining traffic for the Ordnance Depot became increasingly sporadic until final closure.

During the singling of the line at Hadley the opportunity was taken to reroute a local road, so that the road (Station Road) that formerly served Hadley station and a school before continuing towards Leegomery was blocked under the railway overbridge. A new road was constructed about 100 yards to the west, requiring a new railway overbridge, which was built of pre-cast concrete segments, but of only single track width. When viewed from the trackbed today, the narrowing of the trackbed at this point gives a distinctly odd appearance.

Finally, the single track from Stafford Junction to Donnington was closed during 1991 and the track lifted almost immediately.

On the joint SUR/S&BR line from Wellington, the intermediate stations at Admaston, Walcot and Upton Magna all lost their passenger services on 7th September, 1964 on the same day as those on the Stafford to Wellington section. The first two had never offered freight services, but Upton Magna had already lost its freight status on 4th May of the same year and the goods yard tracks were removed before 1966.

Today the SUR can boast 25kVA electrification! Or at least it can for one-third of a mile. Single line track remains *in situ* on the first third of a mile after leaving the Crewe main line at Stafford, complete with electrification masts and catenary. This was installed as soon as the line was closed to facilitate the stabling of civil engineering trains, but has also been used for stabling 'merry-go-round' coal trains from Littleton colliery (now closed) to Rugeley power

One of two original SUR level crossing gates, consisting of cast-iron uprights and gates of bolted metal construction that survive at Derrington. *Author*

station. Alongside a single siding still remains in to the former Universal Grinding Wheel works (now Unicorn Abrasives Ltd). All rail access into the former Bagnall works has been removed.

The trackbed westwards is easy to follow across the open countryside, reaching the M6 motorway, which it passes beneath in a short tunnel. The M6 motorway was built here during the 1960 to 1963 period, at which time the SUR line was still open, of course. Appropriately, during this construction work, a small locally built Bagnall 0-4-0ST (Works No. 2678 of 1942) was used by the contractor J.L. Kier & Co. Ltd on the Creswell viaduct section.

On the other side of the M6, again the trackbed can be followed easily all the way to Gnosall. The crossing keeper's cottage at Derrington is now a private residence, and one of the original metal crossing gates and two cast-iron posts remain on this site. At Haughton nothing remains of the station, although a small picnic area has been provided in the former goods yard area. What was once the nearby Railway Inn is also a private residence.

At Gnosall the bridge over the A518 has been removed, although this did stand for many years after closure. There are no remains of the station, on which site there is now a public footpath. However, parts of the wooden booking office were saved and are incorporated into the new station of the nearby Foxfield Railway, at Blythe Bridge.

All the other over- and under-bridges remain *in situ* on the next cross-country section to Newport, including that over the Shropshire Union Canal, somewhat ironically. Approaching Newport, the line disappears into reclaimed agricultural land, but one overbridge remains isolated in a field, then the line is broken by the alignment of the A41 Wolverhampton to Chester road, as a bypass around Newport.

The interior of Gnosall station booking office in the 1950s. This section of the building was saved from demolition and stored for several years. Most of the booking office is now incorporated into the new Caverswall Road station building of the Foxfield Railway at Blythe Bridge, Staffordshire. *Staffordshire Arts & Museum Service*

The large grain silo in Newport serves as a focal point for examining the railway remains here, with the eastern part towards the bypass having disappeared under industrial development, and the western part up to the original A41 mostly lost under a housing estate. However, part of the station building, conspicuous in its blue-engineered brick, remains as a private residence. Even the road bridge taking the old A41 alignment over the railway has gone, although there is still a bit of a 'hump' in the road at this point.

To the west, the trackbed is once again plain to follow as it curves past the village of Church Aston, across meadows and through Brockton and heads on to a flat agricultural plain to Donnington. The trackbed is once again lost over this flat land, except for the occasional isolated overbridge. At the approach to Donnington, the A518 Stafford to Wellington road has been realigned to actually run on the former trackbed, past the site of Donnington station (of which there are no remains), until it reaches a roundabout just past the old COD Donnington locomotive shed. At this point one can look down on to the disused site of the exchange sidings for the Ordnance Depot. The road then parallels the trackbed to the next, and considerably larger, roundabout at Trench Interchange. However, just before reaching this roundabout a small path can be seen crossing the railway trackbed. Amongst the trees at this point is the site of Trench Crossing station, and the remains of both platforms can still be discerned.

The trackbed is actually in place over the interchange, which was the site of the junction for the industrial Wombridge branch, latterly serving the works of Sommerfelds Ltd (on the site of the original Shropshire Ironworks and Trench Ironworks). Nothing now remains of this branch, nor of the nearby canal, Trench incline, nor any of the ironworks, such has been the total reconstruction with new roads and new factory units. The only slight clue to the Wombridge branch alignment is the presence of the Silkin Way, a 14 mile footpath and cycleway that continues to Coalport, and which at this point uses part of the original branch as well as part of the canal bed. The SUR trackbed continues on to the site of Hadley Junction, now a car park for the employees of the nearby GKN Sankey factory, which still thrives. In this area, it is still possible to trace the divergence of the Coalport branch for a few hundred yards.

A quarter mile further, the trackbed passes the site of Hadley station, now only identifiable by the road underbridge and the adjacent school. The new bridge mentioned earlier, stands oddly on the formation, which continues past Haybridge to the site of Stafford Junction where the S&BR line from Wolverhampton swings in.

The joint line, still fully operational, proceeds in double-track formation to Wellington station, where it is quadrupled through the station. This remains pretty much still in its original condition, and during early 1999 was completely renovated to its original extended condition on both up and down sides. The northernmost platform face on the up island platform is no longer served by rail. The down side bay platforms have been shortened, but are still extant although rarely used, and no longer used for passenger purposes. The engine shed was demolished in the late 1960s and the site is now used by contractors as a track maintenance depot.

Passing out of Wellington, the area is almost unrecognisable. The former GWR goods yard, gasworks and Groom's timber yards on the down side have been replaced by a large supermarket and car park. On the up side, the site of the LNWR goods yard and Smithfield is now similarly occupied by a supermarket and its associated car park. A short distance further on, at the site of Drayton Junction, the divergence of the line to Crewe and Market Drayton can still be discerned, although industrial buildings have encroached thereon.

Now the line passes into open country again, and the site of Admaston station can pass unnoticed, although the station master's house (now painted white) is still extant on the top of the cutting bank. Closer examination of this site also reveals part of the original supporting wall for the rear of the up platform, a gateway at the foot of the steps to the former platform, and beneath the road overbridge lie the remains of the original signal box, booking office and waiting room. These are made conspicuous by a chimney which reaches up on the Shrewsbury side of the overbridge, terminating in a long pipe. At Walcot there is no clue as to the activity that once took place here; only a bare space

A Wolverhampton to Chester 'Sprinter' dmu calls at Wellington station on 30th June, 1999. The bay platform in the foreground was used by SUR Stafford trains starting and terminating here. The locomotive shed was sited on the extreme right of the photograph, beyond the up platform.
Author

A view along the down platform of Wellington station on 30th June, 1999 showing the refurbishment completed earlier that year. Although it is pleasing to note that the through tracks remain, the down platform is no longer in use as an island platform, as only the visible face remains in use.
Author

indicates the site of the former station. The former British Sugar exchange sidings were removed long ago, and much of the land has been acquired by British Sugar, and an associated food company, to expand their production process.

As the line sweeps towards the River Teme, so it now parallels the new A5 route to North Wales, which is an extension of the M54 motorway through Telford. For two miles, the railway and the busy dual carriageway A5 run alongside each other, past the site of Upton Magna station, which has been completely demolished, although an access road and an adjacent overbridge still stand. Finally, the A5 meets a roundabout and turns away, whilst the new part of the Shrewsbury ring road, here designated as the A49 for Whitchurch, now passes beneath the railway which is carried on a new single-span steel girder bridge.

Passing over the graceful curves of the Belvidere bridge over the River Severn, the line now enters the cuttings at the approach to Shrewsbury. There is absolutely no trace of the Potteries Junction and the Potts Yard, but the original goods yards at Abbey Foregate have some identification. The S&BR goods yard on the down side, and adjacent to Abbey Foregate signal box, is now a council road maintenance depot, but the extent of the site can be traced easily. Opposite, blocks of low rise apartments have been built on the site of the SUR goods yard. The extension of this yard, on the western side of Underdale Road, is unused at present, but some building work is planned here soon. The chord line linking with the Hereford line is still in use, as is the massive signal box, and Shrewsbury station is still remarkably unchanged from its last 'modernisation' of the 1960s.

Howard Street goods depot still stands, in commercial use, the former goods yard in front of the depot is now in use as a public car park, and the skew bridge under Howard Street still remains. So, too, does the 1835 Butter Market on one side of the former goods yard, and Shrewsbury Gaol (still in business!) hard on the other side.

In March 2001 a new initiative was announced to reopen three miles of the Wellington to Stafford section. This is to be a partnership between the Ministry of Defence, English Partnerships and the Telford and Wrekin District Council in a £4 million project for a link from the main line at Wellington (Stafford Junction) to the Donnington Base Ordnance Depot, where a new railfreight terminal is to be built. It is hoped that the terminal will also be used by other local industries, and further new rail links are to be explored. However, I understand that GKN Sankey are not interested in re-establishing their one time rail link.

At the conclusion of this review, it is tempting to speculate on what would have happened had the SUR fulfilled its plans and converted its main line canal into a railway from Chester to Wolverhampton. Surely it would have proved a useful freight route (as intended), and a useful diversionary route. However, it is unlikely to have survived the 'Beeching cuts', and so would have been closed. Whereas today this canal is enjoyed by thousands as part of the waterways leisure activity.

There again, it might have been reopened as a heritage steam railway!

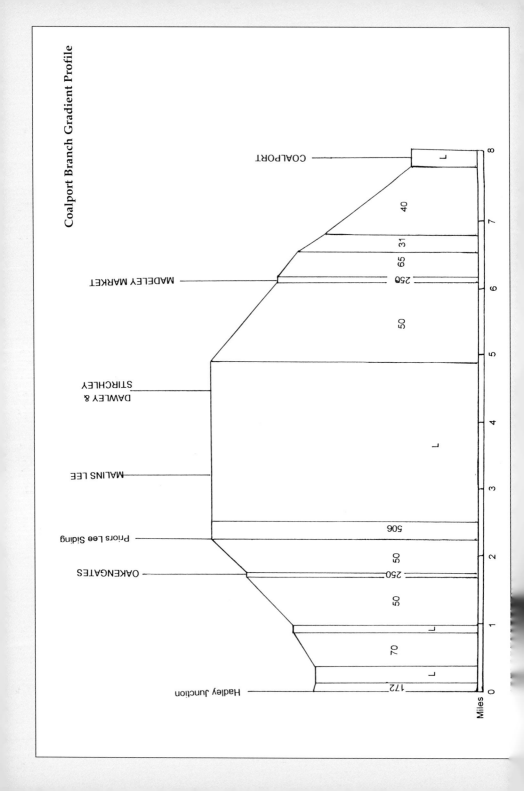

Coalport Branch Gradient Profile

Hadley Junction
OAKENGATES
Priors Lee Siding
MALINS LEE
DAWLEY & STIRCHLEY
MADELEY MARKET
COALPORT

172
L
70
L
50
250
50
506
L
50
250
65
31
40
L

Miles
0 1 2 3 4 5 6 7 8

Chapter Twelve

The Coalport Branch

History and Construction

The history of the Coalport branch starts with the Shropshire Canal, whose enabling Act was passed on 11th June, 1788. Authorised capital was £50,000, and the principal shareholders were Richard Reynolds, the ironmaster John Wilkinson, the Marquis of Stafford, and William Reynolds. The Engineer was John Loudon. The canal was almost entirely opened by 1791, and ran from a junction with the independent Donnington Wood Canal and the Wombridge Canal at the foot of the Donnington Wood inclined plane, to Coalport, with a branch to Horsehay and Coalbrookdale. In this way, it served the principal collieries and ironworks in the area, including the Snedshill and Priors Lee furnaces, the Lilleshall Company's early mines, the Madeley Court ironworks, Blists Hill furnaces and the Coalbrookdale Company.

However, the geology of the area that provided the canal's trade also proved to be its undoing. For the many coal, ironstone, limestone and fireclay mines that littered the area were simply abandoned when worked out. In any case, these mines were never worked to any great depth. The result was considerable subsidence over the whole area. This is particularly serious for a canal, for it results in water loss, which cannot always be rectified immediately. The reservoirs established to maintain sufficient water levels depend themselves on adequate natural local supplies, and these may not always be available in such areas of subsidence, but cannot anyway be expected to cope with any sudden extra demand.

Another effect of the local subsidences was on the structures of the canal. This was particularly important on the Shropshire Canal, as it possessed several inclined planes, notably at Donnington Wood, Wrockwardine Wood, Windmill Farm, Coalbrookdale and Hay Farm. Indeed, subsidence on the Wrockwardine Wood inclined plane was so serious by 1852 that a boat on its travelling carriage could hardly pass beneath the winding drum at the summit.

Almost all of the traffic on this canal consisted of short workings between the various industrial sites of the area, comprising iron, coal, limestone and sand. However, some coal and pig iron was dispatched further afield, notably through the river interchange at Coalport, which grew considerably as a result of this passing trade. William Reynolds, in particular, helped to promote the new village of Coalport and within a few years two potteries, a rope works and a chain works opened there.

The LNWR was granted a 21 year lease of the Shropshire Canal as from 1st November, 1849 at an annual rent of £3,125, and the traffic was fed to the SUR. However, soon there was disturbing evidence of subsidence and in 1853 Robert Skey (General Manager of the SUR&CC, who had been responsible for this canal) recommended to the LNWR Board that urgent repairs were necessary, or that the canal should be converted into a railway. However, this suggestion was rejected. Then, on 1st June, 1854, the GWR opened its branch from Madeley Junction, on the S&BR main line, to Lightmoor. This threatened the LNWR's dominant position in the area, and in the following year Robert Skey again petitioned the LNWR Board. This time his suggestions were heeded and faced with the alternative of repairs costing around £30,000 or building a railway costing £80,000, they opted for the latter.

The LNWR had earlier deposited plans on 30th November, 1852 for a line from the S&BR near to Stafford Junction (at a west-facing junction) to Coalbrookdale, with a branch from this line to Ironbridge via Dawley and Madeley. The engineers were Robert Stephenson and Joseph Locke. However, this was really an attempt to prevent the building of the rival GWR line, and was allowed to lapse when the GWR scheme went ahead. Now a more serious plan was deposited, this time on 29th November, 1856, for converting the Shropshire Canal into the railway as eventually built. The engineers were Joseph Locke (Principal Engineer) and John Edward Errington (Resident Engineer), and the enabling Act was passed on 27th July, 1857. Section 40 of this Act also granted the LNWR the right to purchase outright the Shropshire Canal. Consequently, on 5th February, 1858 the purchase was concluded for the sum of £62,500.

Under the guidance of John Errington, the line was built in two sections. The first was 'LNWR Shropshire Canal Conversion Contract No. 1' dated 18th August, 1858 and let to Daniel Climie of Trinity Terrace, Shrewsbury as contractor, for the sum of £14,958 19s. 11d. Climie's sureties for the contract were William James Clement of The Council House, Shrewsbury and Colin MacKenzie of Wellington. The contract covered the first two miles and 20 chains (2¼ miles) from Hadley Junction to near Wombridge, and was to be completed by 1st August, 1859.

'LNWR Shropshire Canal Conversion Contract No. 2' was awarded on 28th February, 1859 to George Meakin of Birkenhead, for the remainder of the line to the terminus at Coalport for a total of £46,680 2s. 3d. Meakin's sureties were William Wardle, a banker of Chester, and one William Titherington of Dee Mills, Chester. The first section, from a point 10 chains (⅛ mile) beyond the canal tunnel at Stirchley for a distance of 2½ miles was also to be completed by 1st August, 1859. The remainder of the line to Coalport, totalling 3 miles and 20 chains (3¼ miles), was to be completed by 31st December, 1859. However, it appears that both sections overran their target completion dates, such that limited traffic of goods began in the second half of 1860. Difficulties had been encountered in the stabilising of an embankment located between Madeley and Coalport. A considerable number of attempts were made to prevent the infill simply shifting elsewhere and damaging houses, roads and water courses. The stations had not then been completed, so that there was a further delay before scheduled passenger services could begin operation.

The earthworks for the line were laid down as for double track, although the entire line was only ever laid in single track, apart from passing loops mainly at stations. Contractors provided only temporary rails for construction use, the running rails, sleepers and chairs being supplied by the LNWR. No particular problems were encountered in construction, and the only notable engineering feature was a short tunnel near to Blists Hill ironworks.

Proposals were made at various stages to continue the line from Coalport, by means of a bridge, and by way of a junction with the Severn Valley Railway southwards to Bridgnorth and eventually, Worcester. Plans were deposited as soon as 28th November, 1857 by the Birmingham surveyor John Fowler for such a scheme, but nothing resulted. Much later, plans for another scheme, named the Broseley Railway, were deposited on 13th November, 1880 by Edward Wilson. Again, nothing happened, although this is not surprising, as the area was pretty well served by railways by that time.

Opening

Captain Tyler inspected the line in March 1861 for the Board of Trade, and his report dated 30th of that month disclosed several matters requiring attention before approval to operate passenger services could be given. Chief of these was the lack of an operating system for the single line sections, and the total informality governing several sidings which had direct access to the main running line. After a further inspection two months later, Captain Tyler reported on 20th May, 1861 that 'Train Staff' Regulations were to be employed on the single line sections. Control over sidings' access had been improved by the adoption of padlocks in several places, and a bell and arm communication introduced for the signalmen at Oakengates and Priors Lee. His concern over some aspects of bridge construction seems to have abated in the time between the two inspections, and subject to certification of the single line system, he recommended opening of the line for passenger traffic.

The branch had opened for freight traffic, which was always to be its primary activity, around September 1860, whilst passenger traffic commenced on 10th June, 1861. After the inaugural train had run to Coalport, and returned to Oakengates, a dinner was held during the afternoon at the Caledonian Hotel, Oakengates. This event was well publicised beforehand as a public event, which for an all inclusive price of four shillings included 'dinner, ale and dessert'. An account of the opening day appeared in the *Wellington Journal* of 15th June, 1861 but tells us little of the opening trains or of the line itself. Instead, it concentrated on the dinner, and after dinner speeches. The event is noteworthy for the self-congratulatory speeches made by several of the guests, and the toasts mostly made by the chairman, Mr J. Slaney (a local wine and spirits merchant), as follows:

The Queen
Prince Albert
Prosperity to the new line of railway (the Hadley & Coalport Railway)
Success to the LNWR
Success to the iron trade
The town and trade of Oakengates
The Press

and then separately, to each of 15 of the notable guests!

All stations opened on the same day, except for Malinslee which opened for business over a year later on 7th July, 1862.

LONDON AND NORTH-WESTERN RAILWAY.
OPENING OF THE COALPORT BRANCH.

ON MONDAY, June 10th, the Line of Railway between Coalport, Madeley Market, Stirchley (for Dawley,) Oakengates, Hadley, and Wellington, will be opened for Passenger Traffic, and the following Time Bill will come into operation :—

COALPORT TO WELLINGTON.					WELLINGTON TO COALPORT.			
	a.m.	noon.		p.m.		a.m.	p.m.	p.m.
Coalport..................dep.	9 0	... 12 25	...	6 30	Wellington..........dep.	10 20	... 2 0	... 8 0
Madeley Market............	9 8	... 12 33	...	6 38	Hadley............................	10 25	... 2 5	... 8 5
Stirchley (for Dawley).....	9 15	... 12 40	...	6 45	Oakengates	10 36	... 2 16	... 8 16
Oakengates.....................	9 25	... 12 50	...	6 55	Stirchley (for Dawley)...	10 45	... 2 25	... 8 25
Hadley	9 32	... 12 57	...	7 2	Madeley market...........	10 51	... 2 31	... 8 31
Wellington ....arr.	9 40	... 1 5	...	7 10	Coalport ....arr.	11 0	... 2 40	... 8 40

On Thursdays (Wellington market day) an extra Train will leave Coalport at 3 15 p.m. for Wellington, returning from Wellington at 5 15 p.m. calling at all Stations on the line.

First, Second, and Third Class Coaches will be attached to all the Trains.

By Order.

Euston Station, June 1st, 1861.   W. CAWKWELL, GENERAL MANAGER.

Above: Notice of opening and first timetable as published in the *Wellington Journal* on 8th June, 1861.

Right: Notice of opening celebrations as published in the *Wellington Journal* on 8th June, 1861.

Below: Notice of the opening of Malinslee station as published in the *Wellington Journal* on 12th July, 1862.

OPENING OF THE HADLEY AND COALPORT BRANCH OF THE LONDON AND NORTH-WESTERN RAILWAY.

NOTICE.

THE Public are respectfully informed that a PUBLIC DINNER will take place at the CALEDONIA HOTEL, Oakengates, on MONDAY NEXT, the 10th inst., at half-past two o'clock, to celebrate the opening of the above line of railway.

Tickets, including dinner, ale and dessert, 4s. each, to be had at the bar of the hotel.

A suitable train will arrive from Wellington at 2-10 p.m., and from Coalport at 12-50 p.m.

June 7th, 1861.

LONDON AND NORTH-WESTERN RAILWAY.—COALPORT BRANCH.
OPENING OF THE MALINSLEE STATION.

THE above STATION is NOW OPEN for PASSENGER TRAFFIC, and Trains leave Wellington and Coalport as under, calling at all the intermediate Stations :—

ON WEEK-DAYS ONLY.

FOR WELLINGTON—At 8 20 a.m., 12 0 noon, 6 50 p.m., and a Market Train on Thursdays at 3 35 p.m.

FOR COALPORT—At 11 7 a.m., 2 37 p.m., 8 47 p.m., and a Market Train on Thursdays at 5 37 p.m.

All the Trains between Coalport and Wellington are 1st, 2nd, and 3rd Class, and call at Malinslee Station.

For further information see the Company's Time Tables and Books.

By Order.   W. CAWKWELL, General Manager.

Euston Station, London, July, 1862.

Operations

The initial passenger service provided three trains each way on weekdays only, for all three classes of passenger, and calling at all stations. These departed from Coalport at 9.00 am, 12.25 and 6.30 pm; the return services leaving Wellington at 10.20 am, 2.00 and 8.00 pm. All journeys took 40 minutes. On Thursdays (Wellington market day), there was an additional service leaving Coalport at 3.15 pm and returning at 5.15 pm. First class return tickets from Coalport ot Wellington were 2s. 6d., and second class 1s. 9d. By 1897 the service had expanded to three trains each way from Wellington and four from Coalport, whilst by 1905 there were five trains each way, plus two extra services in each direction between Coalport and Oakengates on Saturdays. This was to cater for the Saturday evening markets in Oakengates, which were a popular local entertainment right up until World War II. The 1922 Summer timetable featured an enhanced service of five trains each way, with an extra Saturday return service from Wellington to Oakengates, and the overall journey time was reduced to 35 minutes. Wartime services were reduced to four trains each way, but with the return of peacetime, these were once again improved to five. By 1948 the service had peaked at six trains in each direction, but for its final 1951/52 season this reduced to four, with one extra on Thursdays and two extra on Saturdays.

Goods services were always the mainstay of the line in terms of income, and the 1905 working timetable shows five goods trains in each direction, although not all travelled the entire length of the line. In addition, there were often special goods workings when determined by the needs of customers with rail access. As we shall shortly see, there were numerous private sidings, some leading directly off the single line sections that required a considerable degree of flexibility, not to say ingenuity of working. For example, it was often necessary to attach engines at both the front and rear of goods trains, in order to be able to shunt wagons in and out of customer's sidings. The staple traffic continued to be coal, ironstone and pig iron, as well as bricks and tiles from Blists Hill and Snedshill, and of course sundry freight (which was always considerable) from the goods depots and sidings attached to each of the stations. The LNWR had purchased the large warehouse at Coalport from the Madeley Wood Company in 1857, with the agreement to keep open the interchange from canal to river traffic there. Over the years, the LNWR tended to make such interchange from the river in favour of the railway, rather than the canal, as the River Severn traffic remained sizeable until the end of the 19th century. The warehouse was dismantled at around this time.

During 1955 the line was visited by a Stephenson Locomotive Society railtour, with the Dean GWR 0-6-0 No. 2516 (now preserved at Swindon) as motive power. Other excursions were run from Coalport and Oakengates even after the cessation of regular passenger services. In particular, North Wales seems to have been a popular destination in the 1950s, utilising Stanier 'Black Five' 4-6-0s and 'Crab' 2-6-0s.

As mentioned earlier, the line was single with passing loops, and was worked by the staff and ticket method. The train staff, as authority to proceed on the

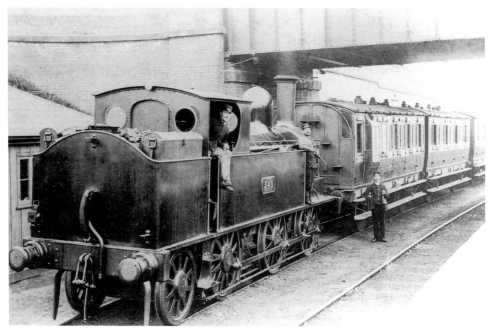

Webb 0-6-2 'Coal Tank' No. 549 (later LMS No. 7550) in plain black LNWR livery, stands in the bay platform at Wellington with a train for Coalport, composed of six-wheel carriages, each with a full lower footboard. The crew are obviously enjoying their pose for the photographer, with the fireman sitting with his leg over the side of the cab, and the driver holding standing on the framing beside the smokebox with his oil can in his hand. The guard is standing beside his compartment, with his watch in his hand. *LNWR Society*

Webb 0-6-0 '18 in. Goods' 0-6-0 No. 8583 at Wellington with a Coalport train on 3rd August, 1935. *H.F. Wheeller*

Webb '18 in. Goods' 0-6-0 No. 28583 storms out of Coalport with a two-coach passenger train for Wellington in September, 1947. These engines were generally only used on goods workings on the line. *Millbrook House/PBW Collection*

A fine view of Fowler 2-6-2T No. 40058 on a branch passenger train to Wellington near Madeley Market on 3rd April, 1951. *R.S. Carpenter Collection*

Shortly before joining the SUR line at Hadley Junction, Fowler LMS class '3' 2-6-2T No. 40048 on a Coalport to Wellington train passes former LNWR '17 in. Goods' 0-6-0 No. 28152 shunting a branch goods train, in April 1949. The Fowler tank is wearing its new BR number, but the 0-6-0 still bears its LMS number. *Millbrook House/PBW Collection*

A busy scene at Oakengates in this view looking north on 30th July, 1932. An ex-LNWR 0-8-0 locomotive can be seen in the goods yard with a rake of wagons while a Webb 0-6-0 heads north towards Wellington with a goods train. *Mowat Collection*

single line section, was issued at Hadley Junction, Oakengates, Stirchley and Coalport. Thus the branch was divided into three sections for operating purposes. Only one signal box was installed *en route*, at Oakengates. At all other locations such as private sidings and station loops, the block sections, points and signals were worked from ground frames, either by the train crew or by station staff.

Description of the Line

The Coalport trains used either of the two east-facing bay platforms (Nos. 3 and 4) at Wellington joint station, alternating with trains for Buildwas, Much Wenlock and Craven Arms. After heading out on the crossover to the up main line, the trains ran in an urban cutting and soon approached Stafford Junction, where they took the left-hand line on to the SUR line, adjacent to the Haybridge ironworks. After a further ½ mile, there would be the stop at Hadley station, located on an embankment, then the train made its way on to the branch proper, forking right at Hadley Junction. Here there were a number of exchange and sorting sidings alongside where the line became single. Trains bound for Coalport had been up trains from Wellington to Hadley Junction, but somewhat confusingly from here onwards were known as down trains. During the next ¼ mile, there were three separate sites where Blockley's brick and tile works had its own sidings from 1897 onwards. After one mile, there was a junction (still on single track) for a spur to Wombridge ironworks and to a wharf on the Trench branch of the SUR&CC. This branch had replaced, in 1873, the original extension of the 'Wombridge Branch' from the SUR at Trench to the Wombridge Iron Works. The line was now running across a mixture of industrial landscape and scrub, and climbing on a 1 in 50 gradient. A ballast tip siding existed on the right from 1912 until World War II, then just past the 1¼ milepost was a siding on the left to Wombridge Old Quarry, which was taken out of use in 1902. At 1½ miles, the line doubled as it ran over the level crossing protecting Station Hill and entered Oakengates station. The crossing signal box was sited on the down platform, with the main station building on the adjacent up platform and comprising a two-storey brick building with slated roof. In front of this building, and actually on the station platform, was an attached single-storey building, containing the booking office and waiting rooms. This had two square bays, which were linked by a wood and glass enclosure, through which access was gained to the platform. Both buildings featured heavy quoins. A separate brick-built gents toilet was provided nearby. This style of building was repeated at the stations for Coalport, Madeley Market and Stirchley (although the latter did not include the wood and glass enclosure). The reason for this commonality of style is that all of these stations were erected by Christopher Baguley, a builder of Madeley who was subcontracted with this work. He later went on to achieve some degree of local fame, as landlord of the All Nations public house, renowned for its own brewed ale right up until recent times. Across the line, on the down platform, a simple wooden waiting shelter was provided. Two goods sidings were sited on the down side, but the up side included a sizeable goods

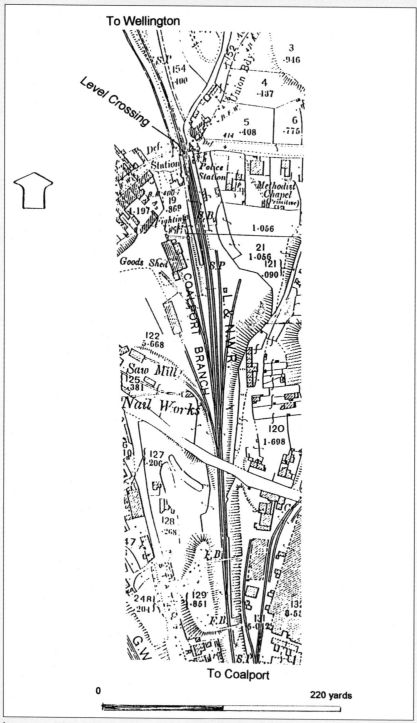

To Wellington

Level Crossing

To Coalport

Oakengates station.

Reproduced from the 25", 1902 Ordnance Survey Map

0   220 yards

The station building on the up platform at Oakengates *c*.1920s. The small signal box is in the foreground on the down platform. Note the splendid building that is the Grosvenor Cinema beyond the station. *Lens of Sutton Collection*

A view along the platform at Oakengates in 1932, looking towards Wellington. The level crossing gates protected traffic on Station Hill. *John Alsop Collection*

A wintry scene, as a Hawksworth '94XX' class 0-6-0PT hustles two coal wagons and a brake van up the grade out of Oakengates with the daily goods working to Stirchley during 1962/63. Access to the Lilleshall Company was via the Priorslee Sidings (*top right*), with the connecting line to the Coalport branch running down the foreground.   *A.J.B. Dodd*

A view from the 2.35 pm passenger train from Coalport as it approaches Oakengates. The train engine is Fowler '3P' 2-6-2T No. 40058. The photograph was taken on 31st May, 1952, the last day of passenger services on the branch.   *T.G. Wassell*

yard and goods shed. In addition, there was a separate timber yard and goods shed for the local company of Millingtons. Oakengates station was renamed Oakengates Market Street for the brief period from 18th June, 1951 until closure a year later.

After easing to 1 in 250 through Oakengates, the gradient stiffened to 1 in 50 once more as the line climbed to cross the S&BR Wolverhampton line, which at this point is in a tunnel. At the same time, the interchange sidings with the Lilleshall Company were reached, located on the left side of the line. Principal traffic emanating here was pig iron and steel from the Priors Lee furnaces and rolling mills (and earlier from the furnaces at Snedshill), plus coal from their Stafford, Lawn, Dark Lane and Woodhouse pits. The line then ran parallel to the S&BR line for a quarter of a mile, albeit at a higher level, then as the gradient eased to level, passed a down siding for the Hollinswood Eagle Iron Company, whilst on the right a further siding was once used for the Stirchley Coal & Iron Company.

Now moving into a semi-rural style of countryside, the line approached Malins Lee station (3¼ miles), located on the up side. No passing loop was provided here. The station architecture was slightly different to other stations, for although the main building was once again two-storey brick-built with slated roof, it was built nearer to the platform so that the waiting rooms and booking hall were incorporated into the main structure and also extended to two storeys. Whilst this part displayed protruberances at each end on to the platform, these were much shallower than the bay window structures at the other stations. Here, as at all stations except Oakengates, the ground frame for working points and signals was mounted on the platform, but the instruments were located in the station offices.

Just beyond the station were two sidings that acted as an exchange with the nearby tramway system that served Dark Lane foundry until 1902. After that date it was used by another local business, Freakley. The line continued on the level, still in rural countryside alternating with industrial premises and relics of the industrial past. On the left was a loop and private siding to Randlay brickworks, which generated a lot of traffic until closure in 1947.

Half a mile further on was the extensive works and internal system of the Old Park ironworks, reached by means of a backshunt off the loop line laid in on the down side. On the opposite side of the line, another loop gave access to interchange sidings with the tramway serving the works of the Stirchley Iron Co. Ltd (which went bankrupt and closed around 1904). This group of sidings, together with another loop a little further on, on the up side was known as Hinkshay Sidings.

At 4½ miles, the line arrived at Stirchley station (renamed Dawley and Stirchley from 9th July, 1923). This featured a passing loop, with the main station buildings on the up side and the usual solitary waiting room on the down side. However, the down side platform and waiting room were removed between 1880 and 1902, although the loop line remained *in situ*. A small goods yard was also provided on the down side, along with a small goods shed; access being from the loop line. After Stirchley, the line crossed the GWR Stirchley branch (still extant) near to the site of the latter's Madeley station.

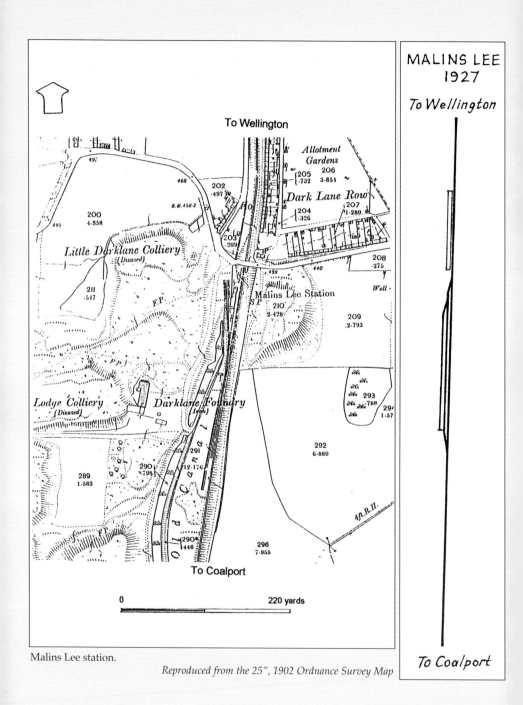

MALINS LEE
1927

To Wellington

To Wellington

Allotment
Gardens
205   206
·732   3·651
202
·497
Dark Lane Row
B.M.458·3   207
200   204   ·1·280
4·858   ·326
Little Darklane Colliery
(Disused)   208
·275
211   Well ·
·517   Malins Lee Station
S.P
F.P.   210
2·428   209
·2·793

293
·788
Lodge Colliery   Darklane Foundry   294
(Disused)   (Iron)   1·57
292
6·880
290   291
·798·   ·12·176
289
1·583
290
·446   296
7·955

To Coalport

0   220 yards

To Coalport

Malins Lee station.

Reproduced from the 25", 1902 Ordnance Survey Map

A view looking towards Coalport of Malins Lee station in 1932. The chimneys on the left are at Randlay Brickworks, and the large chimney on the right at Dark Lane Foundry.

John Alsop Collection

The station master at Malins Lee station *c.*1920.   *Lens of Sutton Collection*

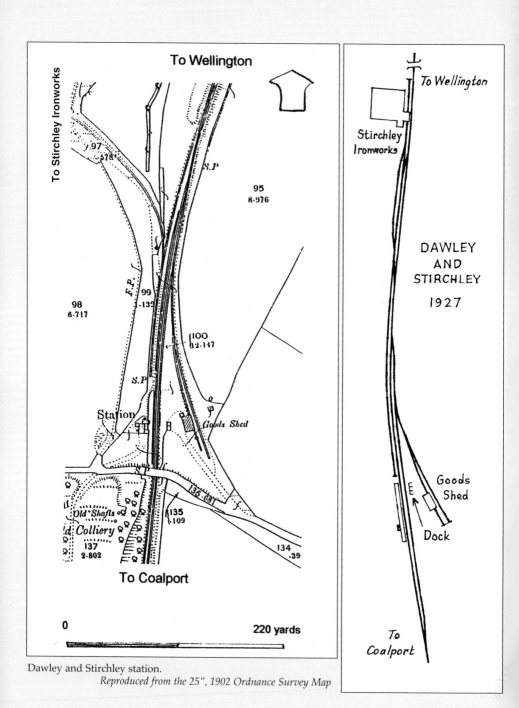

To Wellington

To Stirchley Ironworks

.97

578

S.P

95
8·976

98
6·717

F.P.

99
·135

100
12·147

S.P

Station

Goods Shed

36·081

Old Shafts

Colliery

135
·109

137
2·802

134
·39

To Coalport

0   220 yards

Dawley and Stirchley station.
Reproduced from the 25", 1902 Ordnance Survey Map

To Wellington

Stirchley
Ironworks

DAWLEY
AND
STIRCHLEY
1927

Goods
Shed

E

Dock

To
Coalport

A view looking towards Wellington at Dawley and Stirchley station on 9th August, 1932. The earthworks of the erstwhile down side platform can be seen on the right.   *Mowat Collection*

Shortly after leaving Stirchley, the line began its descent, firstly at 1 in 50 to Madeley Market (6 miles). This was a replica of Stirchley with the main station building on the up platform of the loop line, and a small wooden waiting room on the down platform. Similar to Stirchley, it also lost its down platform, although this is believed to have happened sometime prior to 1890, and the loop line was removed by 1915. The small goods yard and goods depot were located on the up side.

Now running into partially wooded countryside, the line passed the extensive Blists Hill ironworks of the Madeley Wood company. For many years only one small siding on the left of the line gave access to this site, even though it was crossed by tramways at three different points. These connected nearby coal mines to the internal system of the works. However, in 1920 a further siding was added on the down side to give direct access to the brick and tile works. The line had been descending at 1 in 65 from Madeley, but now steepened further to 1 in 31 before plunging into a tunnel, then swinging eastwards alongside the bank of the River Severn. Here the gradient eased a little, but was still a formidable 1 in 40 for almost the entire remainder of the line to Coalport.

At 7½ miles another private siding, this time on the up side was passed, which led to the original Coalport pottery works. However, after the company moved to Stoke-on-Trent in 1926, this siding was taken over by the new factory tenant, the Nu Way Manufacturing Company Ltd, manufacturers of rubber link matting. Finally, at 7¾ miles, the line entered Coalport station (renamed Coalport East by the LMSR, shortly after Grouping), again one of the line's standard station designs, except that here a road overbridge bisected the station area. The single line platform was sited on the down side, giving a good view of the Severn Gorge on a nice day, and the station staff were always very proud that their extensive flower garden put the station into a delightful setting. Alongside the station platform was a two-road carriage shed and next to that the engine shed. Two run-round loops gave access to a small goods yard, and to the goods warehouse alongside the river. During the 1930s a former third class corridor coach was sited in the back road as a camping coach. Its pleasant position overlooking the River Severn was popular with holiday makers. At the buffer stops, the final terminus of the line measured exactly eight miles.

A view along the platform looking towards Coalport at Madeley Market station on 9th August, 1932.
Mowat Collection

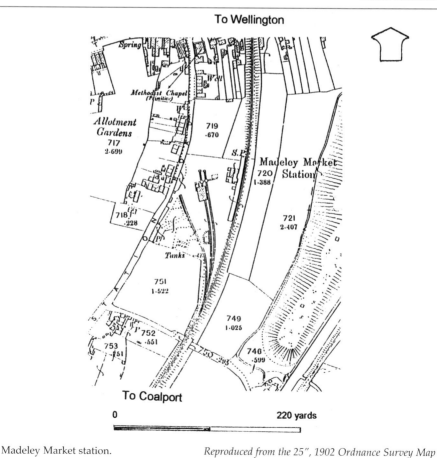

Madeley Market station.   *Reproduced from the 25", 1902 Ordnance Survey Map*

A view down the station approach towards Coalport station *c.*1910. The station master's house abuts the station building and the carriage shed.   *Lens of Sutton Collection*

A view looking north and down onto Coalport station from the road overbridge in 1932.
                                                                John Alsop Collection

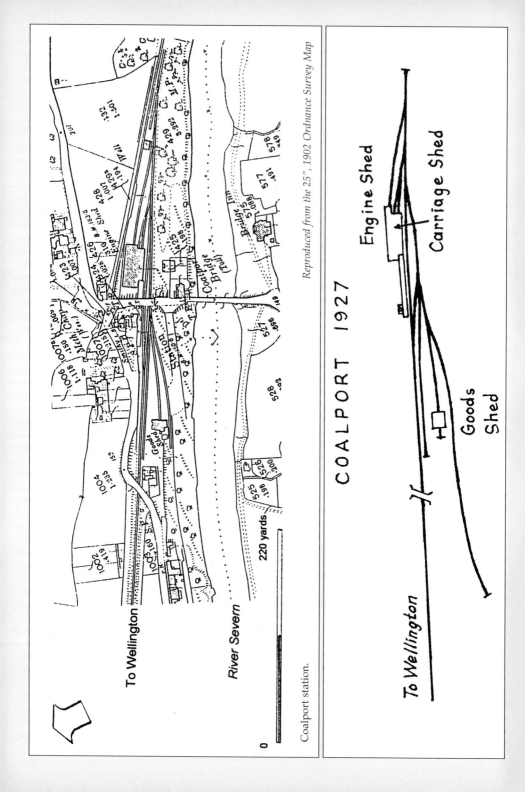

Coalport station.

Reproduced from the 25", 1902 Ordnance Survey Map

To Wellington

River Severn

220 yards

0

COALPORT 1927

Engine Shed

Carriage Shed

Goods Shed

To Wellington

Coalport

Coalport station and yard around 1900, viewed from the southern bank of the River Severn. An LNWR '17 in. Goods' 0-6-0 can be seen shunting the line leading to the goods shed and the site of the former River Severn warehouse.

Shropshire Records & Research

A view looking south of Coalport station on 17th April, 1959 with the carriage shed and water tank beyond the bridge.   *R.M. Casserley*

A view from the Stephenson Locomotive Society special on 23rd April, 1955 looking towards a rather overgrown goods yard at Coalport. The train engine was GWR 'Dean Goods' 0-6-0 No. 2516.   *H.F. Wheeller*

Two views of the station building at Coalport. The view above is believed to date from the 1930s. The picture below was taken on 17th April, 1959.   *Lens of Sutton Collection and R.M. Casserley*

Webb 18 in. 0-6-0 No. 28583 prepares to leave Coalport with a two-coach passenger train to Wellington in September 1947. The coaches are believed to have been LMS conversions of much earlier stock.   *Millbrook House/PBW Collection*

Webb '910' class or 5 ft 6 in. 2-4-2T No. 6757 stands in Coalport station ready for departure to Wellington in September 1947 with the usual antique two-coach set.

Millbrook House/PBW Collection

Fowler '3P' 2-6-2T No. 40058 waits to leave Coalport with the branch passenger train *c*.1951.
Lens of Sutton Collection

The end of the line at Coalport on 17th April, 1959. *R.M. Casserley*

Ex-LNWR 'Coal Engine' 0-6-0 No. 28152 at Hadley Junction in April 1949.   *Millbrook House*

This two-coach set will form the next train to Wellington at Coalport in September 1947, and seemed to have been used on most of the post-World War II passenger services. The first coach (believed to be M22640) was built in 1921 by joining two 28 ft four-wheeled vehicles on a new underframe to become an arc-roofed brake third.   *Millbrook House*

Locomotives and Rolling Stock

Early passenger trains are known to have been worked by cabless Ramsbottom 0-6-0 saddle tanks, known as 'Special Tanks' (actually a saddle tank version of his ubiquitous 'DX' 0-6-0 goods engines). Passenger stock during the 19th century was generally of old four-wheeled stock, without continuous brakes. However, this stock was replaced before 1900 by later vehicles with continuous brakes, and was worked by Webb 2-4-2 tanks, colloquially known as 'Watford Tanks'. In 1905, the passenger services were placed in the hands of steam railmotors of two coach configuration, which were converted from 50 ft arc roof non-corridor bogie stock. These continued to work the line, except when larger trains were required, right through World War I and for some time after the Grouping. Thereafter, the motive power reverted to the 'Watford Tanks' (for example, LMS No. 6757), and various freight types when these were not available. The most popular alternatives were Webb 0-6-0 'Coal Tanks', especially Nos. 7742, 7746, 7755, 27609 and 27664 in the LMS period. But freight was also worked by Webb 0-6-0 'Coal Engines' and 'Cauliflowers' (notably LMS No. 28343), and ex-LNWR Bowen-Cooke 0-8-0 engines. In fact, as Coalport was a subshed of Shrewsbury, anything suitable that was to hand was likely to be rostered. During World War II, it is known that Stanier 'Black Five' 4-6-0 engines visited the line with ammunition and other special trains for storage.

After Nationalisation the 'Coal Tanks' (especially Nos. 58904 and 58926, the latter now preserved) and 'Watford Tanks' (especially Nos. 46757 and 46601) continued, but were further assisted by the introduction of former Midland Railway Johnson '3F' class 0-6-0 goods engines. It was not unknown for ex-GWR Collett '57XX' class 0-6-0 pannier tanks to be made available for passenger work by Shrewsbury Shed. However, following the transfer to WR administration as from 2nd April, 1950, Shrewsbury was allocated four Fowler LMS '3MT' class 2-6-2 tanks, Nos. 40005, 40008, 40048 and 40058. These thereafter regularly worked the passenger trains over the branch, with the latter being a notably frequent visitor. In fact, it worked the very last passenger train over the branch, on 31st May, 1952. At this time Coalport Shed was staffed by two sets of men for the passenger service, and a third set for the morning branch goods.

Rolling stock latterly consisted of an eclectic mix of venerable LNWR and L&Y vehicles, usually well past their prime.

After the cessation of passenger services, the freight workings continued, some of the through workings still being worked by Shrewsbury ex-LMS engines, or even visiting ex-LMS goods engines from as far afield as Burton and Saltley. Although the Collett '57XX' class pannier tanks from Wellington Shed were often employed on the branch 'pick-up' goods workings, some of the more modern Hawksworth '94XX' class pannier tanks were used on through workings from Shrewsbury, especially Nos. 8449, 9470 and 9472.

Closure and After

Following the withdrawal of passenger services on 31st May, 1952, there were up to six goods trains each weekday on the branch. Five originated or

Fowler '3P' 2-6-2T No. 40058 waits with the 2.35 pm for Wellington at Coalport on 31st May, 1952. This was the last day of passenger services on the line and the engine is adorned with a wreath and black flags.   *T.G. Wassell*

A view of No. 40058 at Wellington having just arrived with the 2.35 pm from Coalport on 31st May, 1952.   *T.G. Wassell*

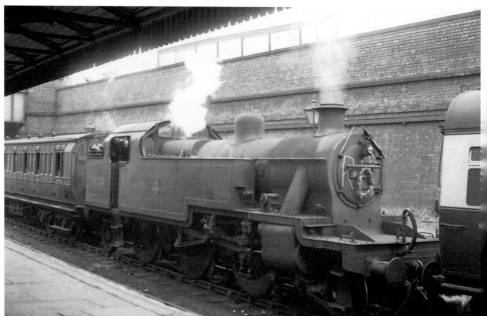

terminated from the Lilleshall Company's exchange sidings at Priors Lee, near to Oakengates station. Two were for Stafford (one morning and one afternoon each way), two for Coton Hill, Shrewsbury (one morning and one afternoon each way), and one at 6.00 pm for Wellington only. This traffic consisted of coke inwards, with steel bar, girders, bricks and concrete products outwards. The sixth working was a purely local 'pick-up' service calling at Coalport, Stirchley and Oakengates goods yards, plus other private sidings as required, such as the scrapyard at Oakengates, and Blockley's brick and tile works. As will be seen from the 1954 Working Timetable, following as *Appendix Seven*, the freight services by this time had dwindled to one through pick-up goods service to and from Coalport, and one morning and one afternoon service calling at Oakengates and Priors Lee Siding. The branch suffered a further blow, when the freight services were withdrawn between Coalport and Stirchley as from 5th December, 1960 and this section was therefore closed completely. However, there was one surviving branch goods working to Stirchley each morning (reporting number 9T69), which originated from Shrewsbury, Coton Hill (at 5.30 am), and returned there (departing from Hadley Junction at 9.38 am). The remainder of the branch from Stirchley to Hadley Junction was finally closed as from 6th July, 1964. The track was soon removed, Ivatt 2-6-0 No. 46524 being noted on this duty in November 1964. However, the sidings at the Hadley end of the branch were used for wagon storage for some time after the branch itself had closed.

Today, much of the Telford area has been landscaped with railways, canals, houses and factories all disappearing to be replaced by new roads, housing estates, offices, industrial parks of brightly clad factory units and vast new retail centres. The effect has been to change completely the landscape hereabouts, and so trying to find evidence of this branch is particularly difficult, although surprises do remain.

At Hadley Junction, as already mentioned, the earthworks of the branch can be traced from the employee car park of GKN Sankey Ltd, curving away for about ¼ mile. Thereafter, the line is lost until Oakengates, where the only trace is the former goods shed, standing alone, and in commercial use. A little further on, a bridge parapet remains, then again the line is totally lost until Stirchley station site is reached. Here the trackbed forms part of the Silkin Way, a cycle and footpath route opened by Lord Silkin on 1st April, 1977. There is no trace of Stirchley station, but at least the trackbed is visible through the recent growth of scrub and trees, and this continues until we reach Madeley Market station. Almost unbelievably, the main station building is still standing, and has been totally restored, although not back to exactly original condition. It belongs to Telford and Wrekin Council, and is in use as an employment centre for disabled persons. Shortly after, the trackbed has been taken over by a road until it emerges on the other side of the road near to the entrance to Blists Hill Open Air Museum, once again as part of the Silkin Way. The short tunnel here has been partly filled in, so that it is only around half as tall internally as it was originally. The trackbed then continues in its new role to Coalport, where all of the station buildings, goods shed, carriage shed and engine shed have been demolished. Even the two road overbridges here are not the originals, although these replacements have been sympathetically designed.

The Stephenson Locomotive Society special 'The Shropshire Railtour' has just arrived tender-first at Coalport on 23rd April, 1955. The train engine, 'Dean Goods' 0-6-0 No. 2516 stands alongside the carriage shed.   *H.F. Wheeller*

Having run-round its train 'Dean Goods' No. 2516 waits to leave Coalport while the passengers make their way back to the train to re-embark, 23rd April, 1955.   *H.F. Wheeller*

The Stephenson Locomotive Society's special, 'The West Midlands Railtour', included a trip down the Coalport branch on 12th September, 1959. The motive power provided came in the form of a Western Region three-car Swindon Cross-Country set. In this scene at Coalport we see the station becoming slowly overgrown. *Lens of Sutton Collection*

Another view of the same railtour as the train approaches Hadley Junction *en route* to Wellington. *Michael Mensing*

A view of an overgrown Oakengates station *c.1962* from the level crossing looking towards Coalport.   *(Both) Lens of Sutton Collection*

Coalport station being redeveloped. A pipeline has been constructed and stands on the trackbed at Coalport, 25th November, 1969.   *RCTS Collection*

Madeley Market station viewed from the site of the platform and seen in a sorry state on 25th November, 1969. *RCTS Collection*

Madeley Market station building on 8th May, 2002. The station is now being used as an employment centre for handicapped persons. *Author*

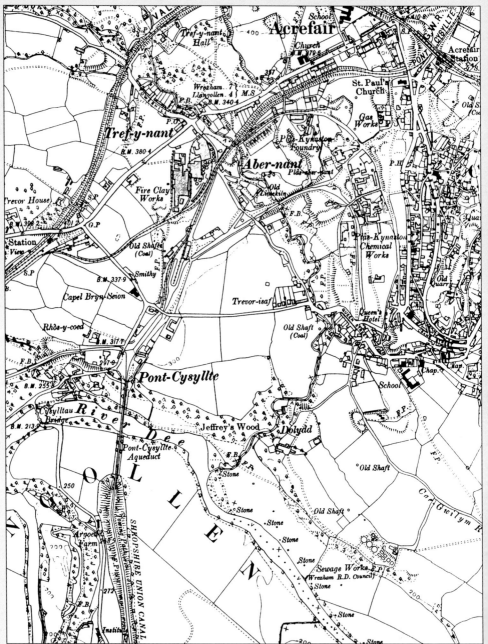

The southern end of the Pontycysyllte Tramway as shown on the 6 in. Ordnance Survey map of 1914. By this date the tramway had been in the hands of the GWR for some 18 years. At the bottom we see the Shropshire Union Canal heading due north over Pontcysyllte aqueduct, which carries it over the River Dee to Pontcysyllte Basin. The tramway runs from the basin and serves a number of industrial sites to the north and north-east. At Acrefair a bridge carried the GWR's Ruabon-Dolgelly over the tramway. The tramway was linked with the GWR system at Trevor Junction, just south of Trevor station (*on the extreme left*) on the Dolgelly line, Plas Madoc Loop Junction on the Plas Madoc branch from Ruabon and, to the north, Rhos on the branch from Rhos Junction and Wrexham.

Chapter Thirteen

Shropshire Union Tramways

The Pontcysyllte Tramway

The SUR&CC did build and operate one other railway: the Pontcysyllte Tramway, otherwise known as the 'Ruabon Brook Tramroad'. This ran from the SUR&CC Llangollen Canal wharf at Pontcysyllte, near Ruabon, for just 3¼ miles to local pits and ironworks in the Acrefair area.

The tramway was originally built for the Ellesmere Canal Company under an Act dated 29th June, 1804 and opened on 26th November, 1805. The tramway was constructed by William Hazeldine as a plateway, and although known to have been of a narrow gauge, the dimensions are not now known. It was intended as a feeder to the canal from William Hazeldine's Plas Kynaston Colliery, but was extended to Acrefair Ironworks and Colliery and then to Plas Madoc Colliery in 1808.The following year it was extended further, to Ruabon Foundry, Wynn Hall Colliery, Wynn Hall Spelter Works, and eventually to Ruabon Brook Colliery. Various, even smaller tramways were opened to provide feeder routes to other collieries and engineering businesses in the locale, so that the system became quite complex despite its small size. Eventually, ownership of the tramway passed through the various canal companies (*see Chapter One*) until it became part of the SUR&CC. Traffic was always worked by horses, until the LNWR, as lessees of the SUR&CC, decided to convert it to a proper locomotive worked standard gauge line in 1861. The conversion proceeded extremely slowly, not being completed until 1867.

From its completion the line was at first operated by locomotives of the New British Iron Company, whose Acrefair ironworks produced a large amount of traffic for the line. Then, in December 1870, the SUR&CC took delivery of its own locomotive, which was destined to be the only locomotive it ever owned. This was an 0-4-0 tank named *Acton*, which had been built by Sharp Brothers of Manchester (Works No. 663) in 1850. It had been supplied new to Edward Oakeley & Company, Coed Talon Colliery, near Mold named *Diamond*. It was subsequently sold to the Birkenhead Railway in January 1854 where it became its No. 27. When that railway was absorbed jointly by the LNWR and GWR in 1860, it was taken into LNWR stock as its No. 356 *Memnon*, but was renumbered on to the duplicate list in 1869 as No. 1118 and renamed *Acton*. Prior to its transfer here, it lost its LNWR number (1118) and so is presumed to have been sold to the SUR&CC. However, as the LNWR was leasing the canals and railways of the SUR&CC, and therefore working the line, it may have remained as LNWR property - but if so, it is unlikely that it would lose its LNWR number. This locomotive is believed to have ended its days at Crewe works, being scrapped there in 1883. Subsequently, locomotives from the LNWR capital fleet were used at Pontcysyllte until 1896.

On 12th February, 1896 the line was sold for £51,000 to the GWR, with the exception of lines actually within the Pontcysyllte canal basin, which remained the property of the SUR&CC, eventually passing to the LNWR, then LMSR and eventual Nationalisation. These few canal-side sidings were, however, worked

A view looking south of Acrefair Low Level goods shed on 6th September, 1952 with St Paul's church in the background. The original SUR line down to the canal basin is on the right. Ponycysyllte Tramway was identified by the GWR as 'Low Level' while Acrefair station and facilities on the Ruabon-Dolgelly line were 'High Level'. *R.W. Miller*

A rare view of the 2 ft 4 in. gauge horse-drawn Glyn Valley Tramway prior to 1886 at Glynceiriog. On the left we see a passenger service waiting to leave the terminus. On the right is the New Inn, this establishment changed its name to the Glyn Valley Inn in 1900.

by the GWR as this section was otherwise isolated from the LNWR system. The lines around the basin became increasingly overgrown, and the wharf was disused by 1945. Finally, the rails were taken up in 1953.

The Glyn Valley Tramway

This well known tramway operated near Chirk, and was opened by the Ellesmere & Glyn Valley Railway Company, which had been formed under an Act dated 6th August, 1866. The contract to build the line was let to Elias Griffith in May 1872 and the line opened to freight traffic in April 1873. It was initially built to a gauge of 2 ft 4 in., and ran for a distance of six miles from the SUR&CC basin at Chirk Bank Wharf to Glynceiriog. At this point there was an inclined extension to various small slate quarries.

From its opening the line was operated by the SUR&CC, using horses for traction, until 30th June, 1881. This included a period of passenger services, similarly horse-worked, which commenced on 1st April, 1874 and lasted until 31st March, 1886.

The Ceiriog Granite Co. Ltd took over operation on 1st July, 1881 and in 1887 began reconstruction of the line for steam haulage using a nominal gauge of 2 ft 4½ in. The enabling Act of 31st July, 1885 permitted new lines of one mile from Pontfaen to Chirk GWR station, of 1¾ miles from Glynceiriog to Hendre, and abandonment of the existing Pontfaen to Chirk Bank section. The contract for construction was awarded to H. Croom Johnson of Wrexham, and work began in 1887, being completed during 1889. Subsequently, the tramway was worked by the Glyn Valley Tramway Company, which restarted a passenger service in 1890, this time using its own steam locomotives.

The last passenger service ran on 6th April, 1933 and the last freight working was on 6th July, 1935. The track was removed shortly afterwards, but traces of the line can still be found.

This commercial postcard was issued after closure with the caption 'The Late Glyn Valley Train'. The locomotive, 0-6-0T *Sir Theodore*, was the first delivered to the line in 1888 and was built by Beyer, Peacock. It is seen with a train on the Hendre extension beyond Glynceiriog.

Appendix One

Directors of the SUR&CC
on 3rd August, 1846

Chairman: Hon. Edward James Herbert
                      (Viscount Clive and 3rd Earl of Powis)
                 Hon. George Anson (Lord Stafford)
                 Sir Francis Holyoake Goodricke, Bart
                 Joshua Proctor Westhead
                 William Henry Gregory
                 Richard Barrow
                 Thomas Groves
                 Joseph Grout
                 George Holyoake
                 George Harper
                 George Loch
                 Henry Newberry
                 John Meeson Parsons
                 George Stanton
                 Henry Tootal
                 John Williams

Appendix Two

Early Comparative SUR
Locomotive Mileages

Year ending	Passenger miles	Goods miles	Without load and asssisting
31st May, 1850	108,011	19,574	not known
31st May, 1851	157,990	28,848	not known
31st May, 1852	175,940	36,342	not known
30th November, 1852	175,811	40,003	7,497
30th November, 1853	167,152	46,138	9,588
30th November, 1854	165,090	60,943	15,382

Note that there is an overlap in the accounting periods, due to a change in the period ends, but all mileages are for 12 month periods.

Appendix Three

Further Proposed Railways

Shropshire Mineral Railway

Plans deposited 30th November, 1845 for a line to run from the GJR at Norton Bridge southwards via Chebsey, Newport, Wombridge, and Madeley to Stokesay. The line as proposed was 43 miles and 5 furlongs-long, and was surveyed by Sam Clegg. Nothing more was heard of this unlikely scheme.

Oxford & Worcester Extension, and Chester Junction Railway

Plans deposited 1st December, 1845 for a line from the Oxford, Worcester & Wolverhampton Railway south of Kidderminster via Sutton Maddock, Kemberton, Stirchley, Wellington, Wombridge, and Hodnet to Chester. No Engineer was given, but this scheme was overtaken by events when the OWWR amalgamated with the Worcester & Hereford Railway from 1st January, 1860 to form the West Midland Railway, which was itself leased to the GWR from 1st July, 1861.

Wellington, Drayton & Newcastle Railway

Plans deposited on 30th November, 1861 and 22nd March, 1862 for a line from the SUR/S&BR joint line at Admaston to Market Drayton and Wolstanton, with a branch to Silverdale ironworks and a spur to the LNWR near Madeley (Staffs). The Engineer was John Ashdown. Part of this line eventually formed the Stoke to Market Drayton line built by the North Staffordshire Railway and opened on 19th October, 1863.

Market Drayton & Newport Junction Railway

Plans deposited on 30th November, 1861 for a line of 12 miles 7 furlongs and 4 chains from the above railway at Market Drayton to join the SUR at Newport. The Engineer was John Gardner, and the railway was an independent concern, sponsored by local landowners and gentry, lead by Mr Henry Reginald Corbett of Adderley Hall. It was also supported by the Duke of Sutherland, whose Lilleshall estate would have benefited from the traffic. This was one further attempt to link the recently opened line from Nantwich to Market Drayton (operated by the GWR) to destinations southwards. As this line did not link to the GWR system, it did not receive its backing, and the project never proceeded.

Shifnal, Newport & Norton Bridge Railway

Plans deposited on 29th November, 1862 by a Mr Burchalls for a line starting at a double junction with the LNWR at Norton Bridge to a south-facing junction with the SUR at Pitchcroft (Newport), and a short spur beyond. The line did not appear actually to reach Shifnal. Nothing more was heard of this proposal, which was similar to the original SUR proposed line from Gnosall to Norton Bridge.

Drayton Junction Railway

The small, but well known Wrexham, Mold & Connah's Quay Railway was incorporated on 7th August, 1862 to build a line from Wrexham to the Buckley Railway, which ran to the River Dee. Connah's Quay was not actually reached until 1882. In 1863, the Wrexham, Mold & Connah's Quay Railway agreed to work the hitherto horse-worked Buckley Railway. In the same year, obviously in an expansionist mood, having promoted an extension from Wrexham eastwards to Whitchurch, the Drayton Junction Railway was separately promoted. It was intended to run from a triangular junction at Prees (three miles south of Whitchurch, on the LNWR Crewe to Shrewsbury line) to an end-on junction with the Newcastle & Market Drayton Railway at the latter town. It would pass through no towns *en route*, simply calling at the small villages of Ightfield and Moreton Saye. After Drayton, the line left the Newcastle & Market Drayton Railway southwards, crossing the SUR&CC canal near to the Newcastle turnpike road, then across open countryside to Eccleshall. Continuing southwards, the line paralleled the LNWR West Coast Main Line from Great Bridgeford, before joining the SUR at a junction shortly before the SUR's own junction with the LNWR at Stafford. A spur was also planned to link to the North Staffordshire Railway at Norton Bridge. Rather unsurprisingly, the LNWR strongly objected and the Bill was thrown out of Parliament. No part of the line was ever built.

Wellington & Drayton Railway

Plans were deposited on 30th November, 1863 for this 16½ mile line running from the joint SUR/S&BR line on the western side of Wellington to Market Drayton, and it was backed from the start by the GWR. It opened on 16th October, 1867, and joined the Nantwich and Market Drayton Railway at an end-on junction. It was amalgamated by an Act of 12th July, 1869 into the GWR, which also absorbed the Nantwich & Market Drayton Railway, but not until 1st July, 1897. However, the GWR had been working these lines since opening, and had running powers over the Shrewsbury & Crewe Railway (later LNWR) giving them a valuable line into the heart of the LNWR at Crewe. Both these lines also made a junction at Market Drayton with the North Staffordshire Railway's line to Stoke.

Newport and Four Ashes (Light) Railway

Plans deposited 4th November, 1922 by the inimitable Colonel Holman F. Stephens of Tonbridge. The line was to run southwards from a double junction with the SUR at Newport via Wheaton Aston and Brewood to a north-facing junction with the LNWR Stafford to Wolverhampton line at Four Ashes. Flyovers were to be constructed to avoid the use of crossover junctions. However, revised plans were submitted on 15th February, 1924 which abandoned the use of flyovers (no doubt through cost considerations!). These revisions also incorporated a junction at Newport now facing towards Wellington only, and the alignment at Wheaton Aston was taken about one mile further north. Nothing more was heard of this line, which would have served a few small villages and provided no better through route for existing long distance traffic.

Locomotives allocated to Stafford, Wellington and Shrewsbury (Abbey Foregate) Sheds

Stafford

30th November,1855 (Northern Division only)

Trevithick 6 ft 'short firebox' 2-2-2 passenger	33	*Erebus*
	34	*Phoebus*
	37	*Hawk*
	44	*Harlequin*
	54	*Medusa*
	109	*Queen*
	111	*Russell*
	167	*Rhinocerus*
	184	*Problem*
	188	*Colonel*
	192	*Hero*
	224	*Violet*
Trevithick 5 ft 'long firebox' 2-4-0 goods	43	*Vampire*
	133	*Ostrich*
	312	*Tubal*
	328	*Czar*
	336	*Woodcock*
	360	*Theodore*
Trevithick 5 ft 'short firebox' 2-4-0 goods	199	*Castor*
	254	*Theseus*

TOTAL 20

1945

Johnson '2P' 4-4-0	443, 461
Stanier '4MT' 2-6-4T	2537, 2565, 2614
Fowler '3F' 0-6-0T	7294, 7588, 7598, 7606, 7649, 7670
Bowen-Cooke '7F' 0-8-0	8940, 9031, 9091, 9098, 9113, 9144, 9194, 9230
Bowen-Cooke 'Prince of Wales' 4-6-0	25648 *Queen of the Belgians*
	25674 *Scott*
	25725, 25749, 25775, 25787, 25841
Webb 'Cauliflower' 2F 0-6-0	28592

TOTAL 29

1958

Fowler '2P' 4-4-0	40583, 40646, 40678
Fowler '4MT' 2-6-4T	42309, 42323, 42345, 42346, 42347, 42389, 42425
Stanier '4MT' 2-6-4T	42538, 42562
Fowler '3F' 0-6-0T	47359, 47588, 47590, 47649, 47653, 47665
Bowen-Cooke '7F' 0-8-0	48922, 49048, 49081, 49115, 49158, 49198, 49229, 49410, 49446

TOTAL 27

Ex-GWR 0-6-0PT No. 3732 at the coaling stage at Wellington Shed on 13th December, 1958.

Michael Mensing

Wellington

1947

Churchward '33XX' class 'Bulldog' 4-4-0	3417 *Lord Mildmay of Flete*
Churchward '43XX' class 2-6-0	5309, 5332
Churchward '44XX' class 2-6-2T	4400, 4403, 4406
Collett '5101' class 2-6-2T	5127, 5135, 5137, 5178
Dean '2021' class 0-6-0PT	2030
Collett '57XX' class 0-6-0PT	3732, 3775, 5758, 9624, 9630, 9639

TOTAL   17

1958

Collett '5101' class 2-6-2T	4110, 4120, 4158, 5167
Collett '57XX' class 0-6-0PT	3732, 3744, 3760, 4605, 5758, 7754, 9630, 9639, 9741, 9774
BR Standard '3MT' class 2-6-2T	82004, 82006, 82009

TOTAL   17

Shrewsbury (Abbey Foregate) SUR

30th November, 1855

Trevithick 6 ft 'short firebox' 2-2-2 passenger	38	*Camilla*
	191	*Diamond*
	233	*Unicorn*
	234	*Mazeppa*
Trevithick 5 ft 'long firebox' 2-4-0 goods	69	*Python*
Trevithick 5 ft ' short firebox' 2-4-0 goods	252	*John O Groat*
	255	*Precursor*
	298	*Don*

TOTAL 8

Appendix Five

Locomotives belonging to Industrial Sites

The Whyte system of classification is used to describe the wheel arrangements of locomotives, both steam and diesel, unless the wheels are not coupled by external rods. In such cases, where, for example, chains are used, they are indicated by abbreviations such as '4w' (four wheel) or '6w' (six wheel).

The general arrangement of steam locomotives is shown as a suffix to the wheel arrangement, as follows:

T	Side tank
PT	Pannier tank
ST	Saddle tank

The position of the cylinders on steam locomotives are further described as follows:

IC	Inside cylinders
OC	Outside cylinders

Diesel locomotives are described as either:

DH	Diesel hydraulic transmission
DM	Diesel mechanical transmission

The following abbreviations are used for locomotive builders:

AB	Andrew Barclay & Sons Co. Ltd, Caledonia Works, Kilmarnock
Cdf	Taff Vale Railway, Cardiff West Yard Locomotive Works, Caerphilly
DC	Drewry Car Co. Ltd, London
HC	Hudswell, Clarke & Co. Ltd, Railway Foundry, Leeds
HE	Hunslet Engine Co. Ltd, Hunslet, Leeds
HKP	H.K. Porter Inc., Pittsburgh, USA
JF	John Fowler & Co. Ltd, Hunslet, Leeds
Lill	Lilleshall Co. Ltd, Oakengates, Shropshire
MW	Manning, Wardle & Co. Ltd, Boyne Engine Works, Hunslet, Leeds
N	Neilson & Co. Ltd, Springburn Works, Glasgow
NB	North British Locomotive Co. Ltd, Glasgow
NBQ	North British Locomotive Co. Ltd, Queens Park Works, Glasgow
P	Peckett & Sons Ltd, Atlas Locomotive Works, St Georges, Bristol
RH	Ruston & Hornsby Ltd, Lincoln
RS	Robert Stephenson & Co. Ltd, Forth Street, Newcastle-upon-Tyne and Darlington.
RSH	Robert Stephenson & Hawthorns Ltd, Newcastle-upon-Tyne and Darlington
Sdn	Great Western Railway, Swindon Works, Wiltshire
TH	Thomas Hill (Rotherham) Ltd, Vanguard Works, Hooton Road, Kilnhurst, Rotherham.
VF	Vulcan Foundry Ltd, Newton-le-Willows, Lancashire
WB	W.G. Bagnall Ltd , Castle Engine Works, Stafford

British Sugar Corporation Ltd, Allscott Beet Sugar Factory

Gauge: 4 ft 8½ in.

No./Name	Wheels	Cyls	Maker	Works No., Date Built	Dates on site
Lewisham	0-6-0ST	OC	WB	2221/1927	6/1927 to 2/10/1970 (a)
Yorkshire	0-6-0T	IC	HC	1070/1914	1928 to 9/1951
AR18	0-4-0DM		RH	304474/1951	6/1951 to 31/10/1983
D2302	0-6-0DM		DC	2683/	
			RSH	8161/1960	10/1969 to 12/7/1983 (b)

Notes
(a) Now preserved at the Foxfield Railway, Blythe Bridge, Staffordshire.
(b) Now preserved at the South Yorkshire Railway Preservation Society, Wincobank, Sheffield.

GKN Sankey Ltd, Castle Works, Hadley

Gauge: 4 ft 8½ in.

No./Name	Wheels	Cyls	Maker	Works No., Date Built	Dates on site
10	0-4-0ST	OC	P	883/1901	On loan during 1943
4228	0-4-0DM		JF	22932/1940	c.1943 to 21/3/1967
4227	0-4-0DM		JF	22937/1941	c.1943 to 21/3/1967
	0-4-0DH		NB	27414/1954	5/7/1957 to 3/1976 (a)
	0-4-0DM		HC	D843/1954	23/2/1967 to 11/12/1976 (b)

Notes
(a) Now preserved at Telford Horsehay Steam Trust, Horsehay.
(b) Now preserved at Cambrian Railways Society, Oswestry.

C. & W. Walker Ltd, Midland Ironworks, Donnington

Gauge: 4 ft 8½ in.

No./Name	Wheels	Cyls	Maker	Works No., Date Built	Dates on site
Hale	0-4-0ST	OC	MW	1055/1888	c.1895 to c.1940
Westminster	0-4-0ST	OC	MW	1343/1897	1914 to c.1952
Becontree	0-4-0ST	OC	HC	1563/1925	1938 to c.1952

Lilleshall Co. Ltd, Oakengates

Gauge: 4 ft 8½ in.

No./Name	Wheels	Cyls	Maker	Works No., Date Built	Dates on site
1 Granville	0-4-0T	OC	N	63/1854	1854 to c.1919
2	0-4-0ST	OC	N	64/1854	1854 to c.1876
3	0-4-0T	OC	N	50/1851	c.1855 to ?

Lilleshall Co. Ltd, Oakengates (continued)

No./Name	Wheels	Cyls	Maker	Works No., Date Built	Dates on site
3 *Phoenix*	0-6-0T	IC	?	c.1859	c.1859 to ?
4 *Constance*	0-4-0ST	OC	Lill	/1865	1865 to 2/1957
5	0-4-0ST	OC	Lill	/1866	1866 to 28/2/1929
6	0-6-0ST	OC	Lill	/1869	1869 to 6/1950
7	0-6-0ST	OC	Lill	/1870	1870 to c.1948
2	0-6-0ST	IC	Lill	/1886	1886 to c.1948
8	0-6-0ST	IC	P	856/1900	22/10/1900 to 5/1932
9	0-6-0ST	IC	RS	1800/1866	c.1904 to 28/2/1929
10	0-4-0ST	OC	P	883/1901	10/7/1901 to 9/1958 (a)
11 *Mercury*	0-6-0ST	IC	MW	995/1886	After 1902 to c.1908
3	0-6-0T	OC	AB	1392/1914	9/1/1915 to 6/1933
11	0-6-0T	OC	AB	1486/1916	27/12/1916 to 7/1959
12	0-4-4T	IC	HC	612/1902	c.1920 to 1934
1	0-6-2T	IC	Cdf	305/1895	5/1932 to 8/1958
3	0-6-2T	IC	VF	1442/1895	5/1932 to 1/1/1947 (b)
5	0-6-2T	IC	VF	1342/1892	7/1934 to 1/1957
2794 *Lilleshall*	0-6-0PT	IC	Sdn	1900/1901	10/1950 to 9/1958
12 *Alberta*	0-4-0ST	OC	AB	1349/1913	12/10/1956 to 7/1959
Prince of Wales	0-4-0ST	OC	AB	1484/1916	12/10/1956 to 7/1959

Notes
(a) Loaned to GKN Sankey Ltd. during 1943.
(b) Transferred to NCB, Granville Colliery upon nationalisation, 1st January, 1947.

National Coal Board, West Midlands Division, Granville Colliery

Gauge: 4 ft 8½ in.

No./Name	Wheels	Cyls	Maker	Works No., Date Built	Dates on site
	0-6-2T	IC	VF	1442/1895	1/1/1947 to 1954
75046	0-6-0ST	IC	HE	2895/1943	5/1947 to 4/1970
	0-4-0ST	OC	AB	2246/1948	1948 to c.12/1967
6	0-6-0ST	OC	Lill	/1869	6/1950 to c.1955
Granville No. 5	0-6-0ST	IC	HE	3771/1952	1952 to 4/1970
The Colonel	0-6-0ST	IC	HC	1073/1914	17/10/1963 to c.12/1966
Hollybank No. 3	0-6-0ST	IC	HE	1451/1921	6/1966 to 7/1968
3	0-6-0ST	IC	HE	3789/1953	6/1967 to 8/1969
8	0-6-0ST	IC	HE	3776/1952	8/1968 to 6/1970 (a)
1D	0-6-0DH		HE	6663/1969	1969 to 11/1979 (b)
2D	0-6-0DH		HE	6664/1969	1969 to 11/1979
6D	0-6-0DH		HE	7017/1971	By 6/1978 to c.7/1979 (c)

Notes
(a) Preserved, currently located at the Embsay & Bolton Abbey Steam Railway, North Yorks.
(b) Currently still in industrial use, at Elf Refinery Ltd, Hebrandston, Milford Haven, Pembrokeshire.
(c) Preserved, and currently in store at Steamtown, Carnforth, Lancashire.

Ministry of Defence, Army Department, Central Ordnance Depot, Donnington
(War Department until 1st April, 1964)

Gauge: 4 ft 8½ in.

No./Name	Wheels	Cyls	Maker	Works No., Date Built	Dates on site
31	0-4-0DM		DC	2158/1941	1941 to 12/1943
1426	0-6-0T	OC	HKP	7540/1943	Not known
1952	0-6-0T	OC	VIW	4425/1943	Not known
75019	0-6-0ST	IC	HE	2868/1943 (a)	1943 to 1/1943 at latest
5065	0-6-0ST	IC	RSH	7101/1943	1943 to 3/1944
75068	0-6-0ST	IC	RSH	7104/1943	1943 to 4/1944 at latest
75157	0-6-0ST	IC	WB	2745/1944	7/1944 to 11/11/1944
75161	0-6-0ST	IC	WB	2749/1944 (b)	8/1944 to 15/11/1944
5093	0-6-0ST	IC	HC	1754/1943	By 9/1944 to 8/1946
71487	0-6-0ST	IC	HC	1763/1944	1945 to 26/8/1945
5117	0-6-0ST	IC	HE	3167/1944	1945 to 7/1946
75171	0-6-0ST	IC	WB	2759/1944 (b)	5/1945 to 11/1945 and 10/1946 to 7/1947
5192	0-6-0ST	IC	RSH	7142/1944	5/1946 to 10/1946
134 (5118)	0-6-0ST	IC	HE	3168/1944 (c)	10/1946 to 6/1951
150 (75186)	0-6-0ST	IC	RSH	7136/1944 (d)	By 10/1946 to 7/9/1954
141 (75144)	0-6-0ST	IC	HE	3195/1944	By 4/1947 to 1953
71531	0-6-0ST	IC	AB	2185/1945	By 8/1949 to 5/1950 latest
120 (71528)	0-6-0ST	IC	AB	2182/1945	1945 to 1950 then 11/1953 to 10/1955
143 (75152)	0-6-0ST	IC	WB	2740/1944	By 11/1953 to 3/1954
105 (75039)	0-6-0ST	IC	HE	2888/1943	By 3/1954 to 1955
115 (75096)	0-6-0ST	IC	HC	1759/1944	On 27/7/1954
138 (75133)	0-6-0ST	IC	HE	3183/1944 (d)	By 12/1957 to 1958
104 (75033)	0-6-0ST	IC	HE	2886/1943	By 3/1958 to 1963
187 (75292)	0-6-0ST	IC	VF	5282/1945	By 9/1960 to 11/1960 latest
429 (8223)	0-6-0DH		RH	466618/1961	1961 to 14/5/1973
430 (8224)	0-6-0DH		RH	466621/1961	1961 to 15/12/1975 and 23/8/1976 to 29/4/1982
431 (8225)	0-6-0DH		RH	466622/1962	1962 to 8/11/1973
224	0-4-0DM		VF	5259/	
			DC	2178/1945	12/11/1973 to 14/12/1983
434	0-6-0DH		RH	469044/1963	16/1/1974 to 5/9/1985
405	0-4-0DH		NBQ	27426/1955	15/12/1975 to 2/7/1976
427	0-6-0DH		RH	466616/1961	25/6/1976 to 16/7/1981 then 29/4/1982 to 14/9/1991
420	0-6-0DH		RH	459515/1961	16/7/1981 to 9/10/1991
433 *City of Nottingham*					
	0-6-0DH		RH	468043/1963	8/10/1981 to 5/6/1985
432	0-6-0DH		RH	466623/1962	3/6/1986 to c.9/1992
256 *Marlborough*					
	4wDH		TH	274v/1977	31/10/1989 to 5/4/1991
253	4wDH		TH	271v/1977	8/6/1990 to 27/3/1991
254	4wDH		TH	272v/1977	10/10/1990 to 20/12/1990

Vanguard 4w diesel-hydraulic *Army 254* (Thos Hill 272v of 1977) undergoing minor repairs in the locomotive shed at COD, Donnington during 1990.   *P. Bushell*

Ministry of Defence, Army Department, Central Ordnance Depot, Donnington (War Department until 1st April, 1964)

Gauge: 2 ft 0 in.

No./Name	Wheels	Cyls	Maker	Works No., Date Built	Dates on site
	4wDM		HE	2226/1940	1940 to c.1957
	4wDM		HE	2227/1940	1940 to 5/1956

Many locomotives (both standard gauge and narrow gauge) were delivered to Donnington for storage only. The above lists cannot be regarded as complete, as many movements, especially during World War II, would have gone unnoticed. As regards these two narrow gauge locomotives, there is no evidence that they actually performed any work during their long stay here.

Notes
(a) Preserved; now located at Rutland Railway Museum, Cottesmore.
(b) Preserved; now located at Caledonian Railway Ltd., Bridge of Dun, Angus.
(c) Preserved; now located at Embsay & Bolton Abbey Steam Railway, Embsay, North Yorks.
(d) Preserved; now located at Peak Rail Ltd, Darley Dale, Derbyshire

Working Timetable for Stafford to Shrewsbury, 30th September, 1954

WEEKDAYS WORKING TIMETABLE - B.R. (L.M.R.) 30 September 1954 until further notice.

Working / Class / Duty no.		Freight H (MX to Coton Hill)	Freight F (MX 9.30pm Burton to Swansea)	Passenger A (MO)	ECS C (MO)	Mails A (MX)	Freight H (MX to Coton Hill)	Freight E (SO 11.40pm Monument Lane to Harlescott Sdgs)	Freight H	Passenger B	Freight K 108	Passenger B	Passenger B	Freight H (to Swansea)	Freight H (7.45 from Branston RAR)
Stafford	dep.	12.10am	12.50	1.00		2.10 Not advertised G	4.00	4.50	5.15	6.05	6.20	7.20	8.55	9.25	10.30
Haughton	arr.														
	dep.														
Gnosall	arr.														
	dep.														
Newport	arr.	12.40								6.16	6.50	7.31	9.06		
	dep.									6.24		7.39	9.14		
Donnington	arr.			1.26						Not advertised	8.35	7.40	9.15		
	dep.			1.30	1.50	2.27					8.45	7.45 1/2	9.20 1/2		
Trench Crossing	arr.										9.30	7.50	9.24		
	dep.										9.35 M				
Hadley Junction	arr.			Not advertised							9.50 M	7.54	9.28		
	dep.										9.55				
Hadley	arr.										10.10	7.57	9.31		
	dep.	12.57	1.32				4.55	5.32	6.02			7.59	9.32	10.30	11.17
Wellington (passenger)	arr.				2.00	2.39						8.03	9.36		
	dep.					2.50						8.09	9.42		
Wellington (goods)	arr.	1.05	1.42		to work 5.10am to Donnington		5.05							10.40	11.30
	dep.	1.12	2.08				5.15	5.43			10.19				
Admaston	arr.														
	dep.														
Walcot	arr.											8.13	9.46		
	dep.														
Upton Magna	arr.							6.00					9.50 1/2	10.49 N	
	dep.							6.36				8.18	9.52	11.05 N	
Abbey Foregate	arr.	1.38	2.29				5.40	6.44					9.56 1/2		
	dep.	1.53	3.10				5.43					8.23	9.58		
Coleham	arr.	2.03												11.20	11.52
Shrewsbury General	arr.		3.15/3.30			3.05		6.47				8.30	10.05	11.30	11.57

Notes:

G — Stops for postal services and to set down Military personnel.   Conveys newspapers FSO, and departs Stafford at 2.10am.

M — At Donnington no.3 Box

N — At Allscott Sugar Works Sidings.

WEEKDAYS

WORKING TIMETABLE - B.R. (L.M.R.) 30 September 1954 until further notice.

Station		Freight K 70 (am)	Lt. Engine G 70 (pm)	Freight K 69 (pm)	Passenger B (pm)	Freight H (6.25am Annesley to Pontypool Road)	Freight K 117 SX	ECS C FO	Passenger B (pm)	Freight H To Swansea SX	Freight H To Swansea SO	Passenger B	Freight F 69 SX	Lt. engine G 117 SX
Stafford	dep.	10.50			1.04	1.16		3.25	3.42	3.55	4.05	5.35		
Haughton	arr.	11.04												
Haughton	dep.	11.14												
Gnosall	arr.													
Gnosall	dep.	1.24			1.15				3.53			5.46		
Newport	arr.	11.40			1.23				4.01			5.54		
Newport	dep.	11.55			1.24			3.45	4.02			5.55		
Donnington	arr.	12.02pm	After working		1.24				4.07 1/2			6.00 1/2	6.10 M	
Donnington	dep.	12.12	11.30 from Donnington		1.31				4.10			6.03		
Trench Crossing	arr.	12.30					3.00		4.13 1/2			6.07		
Trench Crossing	dep.	12.35 M			1.35									
Hadley Junction	arr.	12.55 M				2.01	3.10		4.16	4.42	4.52		6.15	6.35
Hadley	arr.				1.38				4.19			6.10		
Hadley	dep.	1.10	12.15pm	12.42 Q	1.39				4.20			6.11		
Wellington (passenger)	arr.				1.43			3.58 to work 5.20pm to Stafford	4.25			6.15		
Wellington (passenger)	dep.		12.20		1.46				4.28					6.40
Wellington (goods)	arr.					2.14					5.00			
Wellington (goods)	dep.			1.05						4.50				
Admaston	arr.				1.50				4.31 1/2					
Admaston	dep.				1.51				4.33					
Walcot	arr.				1.56				4.37 1/2		5.09 N			
Walcot	dep.				1.57				4.39		5.18 N			
Upton Magna	arr.				2.02				4.43 1/2					
Upton Magna	dep.				2.03				4.45					
Abbey Foregate	arr.									5.15				
Abbey Foregate	dep.													
Coleham	arr.					2.34								
Coleham	dep.		12.40			2.39				5.36	5.36			
Shrewsbury General	arr.		12.46		2.10				4.52	5.39	5.39			

Notes:
M At Donnington No.3 Box.
N At Allscott Sugar Works Sidings.
Q At Haybridge Sidings. arr. 12.47pm, dep. 1.00pm.

WORKING TIMETABLE - B.R. (L.M.R.) 30 September 1954 until further notice.

WEEKDAYS

Station	arr./dep.	Passenger B	Freight H 69 to Harlescott Sidings	Freight H SX to Swansea SO to Llandovery	Passenger B	Freight H 5.15pm from Branston SO	Passenger B	Freight H 7.33pm Tamworth to Harlescott Sidings SX	Freight J 5.55pm from Bescot SX	Freight J SO	Freight H (RAR) 8.43pm Tamworth to Harlescott Sidings SX
Stafford	dep.	6.22			8.22	8.36	9.29	10.10	10.48	11.20	11.35
Haughton	arr.										
	dep.			7.15							
Gnosall	arr.				8.33						
	dep.	6.33			8.35		9.40				
Newport	arr.	6.41			8.43		9.48				
	dep.	6.43			8.45		9.50				
Donnington	arr.	6.48 1/2			8.50 1/2						
	dep.	6.53			8.53		9.56				
Trench Crossing	arr.										
	dep.										
Hadley Junction	arr.			8.02						12.17am	
	dep.	6.57	7.50	8.28	8.57	9.25	10.00	10.57	11.42	12.21	12.22am
Hadley	arr.	7.00			9.00		10.03				
	dep.	7.01			9.01		10.04				
Wellington (passenger)	arr.	7.05			9.05		10.08				
	dep.	7.10					10.13				
Wellington (goods)	arr.										
	dep.		8.00	8.36		9.38		11.05	11.51	12.30	12.30
Admaston	arr.										
	dep.										
Walcot	arr.										
	dep.										
Upton Magna	arr.					9.55					
	dep.					10.04					
Abbey Foregate	arr.					10.14					
	dep.										
Coleham	arr.										
	dep.		8.25	9.04		10.23		11.29	12.15am	12.58	12.54
Shrewsbury General	arr.	7.34	8.28	9.09		10.27	10.28	11.39 S	12.21	1.05	12.57 T

SUNDAYS

Station	arr./dep.	Freight F 9.10pm from Burton	Freight H to Harlescott Sidings	Passenger B	Passenger B	Passenger B
Stafford	dep.	12.37am	1.00am	11.00	6.50pm	9.30
Haughton	arr.					
	dep.					
Gnosall	arr.					
	dep.			11.11	7.01	
Newport	arr.			11.19	7.09	
	dep.			11.20	7.10	
Donnington	arr.			11.25 1/2	7.15 1/2	9.55
	dep.			11.27	7.17	10.00
Trench Crossing	arr.					
	dep.					
Hadley Junction	arr.					
	dep.	1.19	1.51	11.31	7.21	10.03 1/2
Hadley	arr.			11.34	7.24	
	dep.			11.35	7.25	10.08
Wellington (passenger)	arr.			11.39	7.29	10.15
	dep.					
Wellington (goods)	arr.					
	dep.	1.27	2.01			
Admaston	arr.					
	dep.					
Walcot	arr.					
	dep.					
Upton Magna	arr.					
	dep.					
Abbey Foregate	arr.					
	dep.					
Coleham	arr.		2.26			
	dep.	1.51	2.37			
Shrewsbury General	arr.	1.56	2.41			

Notes:

S   Does not run when 8.43pm from Tamworth runs.
T   Runs when 5.55pm SX Euston to Manchester (RAR) runs.

WORKING TIMETABLE - B.R. (L.M.R.) 30 September 1954 until further notice.

WEEKDAYS

Station	dep./arr.	Freight F · to Burton N.Staffs Junction · SO	Passenger A · 1.35am from Crewe · MO	Freight F · to Burton N.Staffs Junction · MX	ECS C · After working 1.35am from Crewe · MO	Freight F · to Burton N.Staffs Junction · MO	Freight H · MX	Freight H · 2.22am from Crewe · MX	Passenger B · not advertised · MO	ECS C · After working 5.10am from Wellington · MO	Freight H · MO	Lt.engine G · 69 · to work 5.35am to Coalport	Freight H · 3.08am from Crewe · SO	Freight K · 69 · to Coalport	Freight H · 8.55pm from Swansea · MX
Shrewsbury General	dep.														
Coleham	dep.														
Abbey Foregate	arr.						4.30	4.36			4.55	5.10	5.16		5.27
Abbey Foregate	dep.	1.38am		2.30		3.30		4.40				5.15	5.20	5.35	6.22
Upton Magna	arr.														
Upton Magna	dep.														
Walcot	dep.								not advertised			to work 5.35am to Coalport			
Admaston	arr.		not advertised												
Admaston	dep.														
Wellington (goods)	arr.	2.05												6.01	
Wellington (goods)	dep.			2.55		3.52	4.55				5.22			6.25	6.50
Wellington (passenger)	arr.		2.35												
Wellington (passenger)	dep.		2.45						5.10						
Hadley	arr.				After working 1.35am from Crewe					After working 5.10am from Wellington					
Hadley	dep.														
Hadley Junction	arr.								5.17						
Hadley Junction	dep.	2.11		3.01		3.58	5.01		5.21		5.33			6.31	
Trench Crossing	arr.														
Donnington	arr.		2.52												7.02
Donnington	dep.		2.57		3.05					5.24					7.35
Newport	arr.														
Newport	dep.									5.31					
Gnosall	arr.														
Gnosall	dep.														
Haughton	arr.														
Haughton	dep.														
Stafford	arr.	3.00		3.50	3.35	4.40	5.50			5.50	6.25				8.30

WORKING TIMETABLE - B.R. (L.M.R.) 30 September 1954 until further notice.

WEEKDAYS

Working / Class / Duty no.	ECS C	Passenger B	Passenger B	Lt. engine G · 70	Passenger B	Freight K · 70	Freight H	Lt. engine G · 117	Freight K · 108	Passenger B	Passenger B	Freight H to Burton	Freight K · 117 SX	Passenger B
Shrewsbury General dep.	6.15am									11.28	12.20pm			3.10
Coleham dep.					7.45									
Abbey Foregate arr.														
Abbey Foregate dep.														
Upton Magna arr.				7.25	7.52					11.35				
Upton Magna dep.				7.30	7.53	8.08				11.36	12.27	12.28		3.18
Walcot arr.				To work		8.28 N								
Walcot dep.				8.08 to	7.57	9.15 N				11.41	12.32			3.23
Admaston arr.				Donnington										
Admaston dep.					8.01						12.37			3.28
Wellington (goods) arr.						9.25						12.56		
Wellington (goods) dep.						9.36			11.10					
Wellington (passenger) arr.	6.30				8.06					11.50	12.41			3.32
Wellington (passenger) dep.			7.06		8.08					11.52	12.43			3.38
Hadley arr.			7.09		8.11					11.55				
Hadley dep.	to work		7.11		8.12			10.20		11.56	12.46			3.41
Hadley Junction arr.	7.06 to		7.14		8.15	9.41	10.16	10.25	11.16	11.59	12.48	1.02	1.05	3.42
Hadley Junction dep.	Stafford		7.15			9.51		to shunt					1.10 P	
Trench Crossing arr.														
Trench Crossing dep.			7.18 1/2			9.35								
Donnington arr.						10.10			11.26	12.02 1/2	12.51	1.09	1.55 P	3.45
Donnington dep.			7.22		8.22	10.15 M			11.36	12.05pm	12.54 1/2	1.25	2.00	3.48 1/2
Newport arr.			7.28		8.28				11.50	12.11	12.57			3.51
Newport dep.		7.00	7.30		8.31				1.15pm	12.12	1.03			3.57
Gnosall arr.		7.09	7.39		8.38				1.29	12.21	1.04	R		3.58
Gnosall dep.		7.10	7.40		8.41				1.40	12.22	1.13			4.07
Haughton arr.														
Haughton dep.											1.14			4.08
Stafford arr.		7.20	7.52		8.51		11.07		2.16	12.35	1.24	2.30		4.20
							W					Y		

Notes:

M	At Donnington no.3 Box.	
N	At Allscott Sugar Works Sidings.	
W	Arrives 11.10pm	SO
Y	Arrives 2.41 pm	SO
R	Calls as required.	
P	At Trench Sidings.	

WORKING TIMETABLE - B.R. (L.M.R.) 30 September 1954 until further notice.

WEEKDAYS

Station		Freight H SX	Freight H SO	EBV G 69 SX	Passenger A FO	Passenger B	Freight F	Passenger B	Passenger B	Mail A
Shrewsbury General	dep.					5.50				11.25
Coleham	dep.									
Abbey Foregate	arr.									
Abbey Foregate	dep.									
Upton Magna	arr.									
Upton Magna	dep.					5.57	5.58			
Walcot	arr.									
Walcot	dep.					6.02				
Admaston	arr.									
Admaston	dep.					6.07				
Wellington (goods)	arr.									
Wellington (goods)	dep.						6.20 R			
Wellington (passenger)	arr.					6.11				11.40
Wellington (passenger)	dep.				5.20	6.15		9.05	10.25	11.45
Hadley	arr.				5.23	6.18		9.08	10.28	
Hadley	dep.				5.25	6.20		9.09	10.30	
Hadley Junction	arr.						6.30			
Hadley Junction	dep.	3.50	3.50	5.15			7.07			
Trench Crossing	arr.	3.56 M								
Trench Crossing	dep.	4.08 M			5.29	6.23	Class H from Hadley Junction	9.12	10.33	
Donnington	arr.	4.12	3.58	5.20		6.26 1/2		9.15 1/2	10.35 1/2	
Donnington	dep.	4.19	4.19	To work 6.10pm to Hadley Junction	5.33	6.29		9.19	10.39	
Newport	arr.	4.30	4.30		5.39	6.35		9.25	10.45	
Newport	dep.	4.40	4.40		5.40	6.37		9.26	10.47	11.55
Gnosall	arr.					6.46		9.35	10.56	
Gnosall	dep.					6.47		9.36	10.57	
Haughton	arr.									
Haughton	dep.									
Stafford	arr.	5.14	5.14		5.58	6.57	8.05	9.46	12.07	12.13am

Notes: R — Calls as required. M — At Donnington 3 Box

SUNDAYS

Station		Passenger B	Passenger B	Passenger B
Shrewsbury General	dep.	12 noon	8.14pm	10.45
Abbey Foregate	arr.	12.03pm	8.17	10.51
Abbey Foregate	dep.	12.04	8.18	10.52
Upton Magna	dep.	12.07	8.21	10.56
Admaston	dep.	12.11	8.25	
Wellington (passenger)	arr.	12.17	8.31	11.00
Wellington (passenger)	dep.	12.18	8.32	
Newport	arr.	12.27	8.42	
Newport	dep.	12.28		
Stafford	arr.	12.38	8.52	11.32

There are no Sunday 'up' freight services.

Working Timetable for the Coalport Branch
30th September, 1954

Weekdays Only

		Freight	Freight	Freight
Working Class		H	K	K
Duty no.				69
			Departs 6.25am Wellington	Departs 2.20pm Wellington
		am	am	pm
Hadley Junction	arr.		6.31	2.28
	dep.	6.47	7.45	3.01
Oakengates	arr.	6.57	7.52	3.11
	dep.	7.00	9.12	3.35
Priors Lee Siding	arr.	7.06	9.17	3.40
	dep.		9.22	
Dawley & Stirchley	arr.		9.32	
	dep.		9.50	
Madeley Market	arr.		10.00	
	dep.		10.10	
Coalport	arr.		10.20	

		Freight	Freight	Freight
Working Class		K	J	J
Duty no.			69	69
		am	am	pm
Coalport	dep.		11.10	
Madeley Market	arr.			
	dep.			
Dawley & Stirchley	arr.			
	dep.			
Priors Lee Siding	arr.		11.35	
	dep.	7.15	11.50	3.53
Oakengates	arr.			3.58
	dep.	7.20	11.55	4.10
Hadley Junction	arr.	7.28	12.03	4.25
	dep.			

Appendix Eight

Chronological Table of Important Events

1779	Chester Canal opened
1791	Shropshire Canal opened
1795	'Wirral Line' canal opened
1796	Llanymynech branch of Ellesmere Canal opened (1st July)
1797	Shrewsbury Canal opened throughout
1805	Ellesmere Canal 'main line' opened to Hurleston
1805	Pontcysyllte Tramway opened (26th November)
1806	Prees branch of Ellesmere Canal opened
1808	Whitchurch branch of Ellesmere Canal opened
1808	Llangollen branch of Ellesmere Canal opened
1813	Ellesmere and Chester Canals amalgamated (1st July)
1832	Norbury Junction branch to Shrewsbury Canal opened (12th January)
1835	Birmingham and Liverpool Junction Canal opened fully (2nd March)
1835	Barbridge to Middlewich branch canal opened (1st September)
1845	Ellesmere & Chester Canal, and Birmingham & Liverpool Junction Canal amalgamated (1st May)
1846	Birmingham & Liverpool Junction Canal changed name to SUR&CC (3rd August)
1846	SUR&CC acquired Shrewsbury Canal (3rd August)
1847	SUR&CC acquired Eastern branch of Montgomeryshire Canal (February)
1847	Act passed for LNWR perpetual lease of SUR&CC (July)
1849	Formal opening of SUR, Stafford to Shrewsbury (1st June)
1849	SUR&CC leased Shropshire Canal (1st November)
1850	SUR&CC acquired Western Branch of Montgomeryshire Canal (5th February)
1854	Act passed for GWR acquisition of S&BR (7th August)
1855	Trench Crossing station opened (1st January)
1857	Plans deposited for Howard Street goods depot (30th November)
1860	Coalport branch opened for goods traffic
1861	Coalport branch opened to passengers (10th June)
1862	LNWR/GWR Shrewsbury-Welshpool line opened (27th January)
1862	Malinslee station opened (7th July)
1866	Wombridge goods branch opened
1866	PSNWR line opened, linking to joint line at Shrewsbury (13th August)
1867	'Abbey Curve', Shrewsbury opened for traffic (1st May)
1873	Glyn Valley Tramway opened to goods (April)
1880	PSNWR line closed for second time, link to joint line removed (22nd June)
1881	SUR&CC ceased operation of Glyn Valley Tramway (30th June)
1903	Major reconstruction of Shrewsbury General station completed
1944	Final section of Shrewsbury Canal closed
1945	Remainder of Pontcysyllte Tramway disused
1949	Haughton station closed to passengers ((23rd May)
1952	Coalport branch closed to passengers (31st May)
1957	Haughton closed to goods traffic (5th August)
1959	Lilleshall Company internal railway system closed
1960	Stirchley to Coalport closed to goods traffic (5th December)
1964	Gnosall station closed to goods traffic (1st June)
1964	Hadley Junction to Stirchley closed to goods traffic (6th July)
1964	Stafford to Wellington closed to passengers (7th September)

1964 Admaston, Walcot and Upton Magna stations closed to passengers (7th September)
1965 Donnington station closed to goods traffic (4th October)
1966 Stafford to Donnington closed completely (1st August)
1968 Remainder of Wombridge branch closed completely (27th April)
1971 Wellington to Donnington section singled
1972 Rail traffic ceased to GKN Sankey Ltd.
1979 Last train from NCB, Granville Colliery to Donnington (2nd October)
1983 Rail traffic ceased to British Sugar, Allscott (July)
1991 Rail traffic ceased to MOD, COD Donnington
1991 Wellington to Donnington section closed completely

Stanier '8F' class 2-8-0 No. 48738 passes Gnosall signal box with a Wellington-Stafford freight train on 5th September, 1964.   *Millbank House*

Bibliography & Acknowledgements

The following secondary sources of information have been consulted:

A Regional History of the Railways of Great Britain – Volume 7 – The West Midlands by Rex Christiansen (David & Charles)

Forgotten Railways (Volume II) – Severn Valley and Welsh Border by Rex Christiansen (David & Charles)

Rail Centres: Wolverhampton by Paul Collins (Ian Allan)

Rail Centres: Shrewsbury by Richard K. Morriss (Ian Allan)

LMS Engine Sheds - Volume 1: The L&NWR by Chris Hawkins & George Reeve (Wild Swan)

An Historical Survey of Great Western Engine Sheds - 1947 by E. Lyons (Oxford Publishing Co.)

Encyclopedia of British Railway Companies by Christopher Awdry (Guild Publishing)

The Directory of British Railway Stations by R.V.J. Butt (Patrick Stephens Ltd)

Industrial Railway Record, Nos. 100, 135, 153. (Industrial Railway Society)

Industrial Locomotives of Cheshire, Shropshire and Herefordshire (Industrial Railway Society)

Industrial Locomotives of North Staffordshire by Allan C. Baker (Industrial Railway Society)

Industrial Locomotives of North Wales by V. J. Bradley (Industrial Railway Society)

Bagnalls of Stafford - Locomotive Works List by Allan C. Baker & T.D. Allen Civil (Industrial Locomotive Society)

Continent, Coalfield and Conservation by A.P. Lambert and J.C. Woods (Industrial Railway Society)

The Stafford and Uttoxeter Railway by P. Jones (Oakwood Press)

The Stoke to Market Drayton Line by C.R. Lester (Oakwood Press)

The Wenlock Branch by K. Jones (Oakwood Press)

'The Coalport Branch' by William H. Smith (*British Railway Journal* No. 19)

'Premier Line to Coalport', *Railway Bylines*, April 1999

'Letters', *Railway Bylines*, June 1999

An Historical Survey of the Railways Serving Stafford by A. M. Gully (Journal of the Staffordshire Industrial Archaeological Society, No. 8, 1978)

Track Layouts of the GWR – Section 32, East Shropshire by R.A. Cooke

Gazeteer of the Railway Contractors and Engineers of Central England, 1830-1914 by L. Popplewell (Melledgen Press)

Canals of Shropshire by Richard K. Morriss (Shropshire Books)

Railways of Shropshire by Richard K. Morriss (Shropshire Books)

Canals of the West Midlands by Charles Hadfield (David & Charles)

The Shroppie by Thomas Pellow & Paul Bowen (Landscape Press)

A History of Shropshire by Barrie Trinder (Phillimore)

The Industrial Archaeology of Shropshire by Barrie Trinder (Phillimore)

The Lilleshall Co. Ltd: A History, 1764-1964 by W.K.V. Gale & C. R. Nicholls (Moorland Publishing)

I should also like to acknowledge the assistance of the staff of the public libraries at Stafford, Newport, Telford, Madeley, Oakengates and Wellington, as well as those at Shropshire Records & Research Centre in Shrewsbury, the Staffordshire Records Office and William Salt Library in Stafford, and the Public Record Office in Kew. Thanks must also go to the staff of the Newport and Market Drayton Advertiser, and to Richard Taylor (Curator, Archives Collection) at the National Railway Museum in York, and to John Powell, Librarian at the Ironbridge Gorge Museum Trust, Coalbrookdale. Also thanks to Peter Bushell, Peter Harris, Arthur Leek, Mr A.T. Minor, Ken Webb, George Finney and Cliff Carr for their personal recollections. Ted Talbot and Allan Baker have been particularly helpful. The tickets are from John Strange's collection and are reproduced with permission. I am also grateful for information supplied by the Madeley Local Studies Group. Finally, to my wife Sandra, for her help, ideas, and encouragement.

Index